TORTURED BARRIO SONGS

by

Reyes Cárdenas

Tortured Barrio Songs
Reyes Cárdenas

FlowerSong Books
McAllen, Texas 78501

Copyright © 2019 by Reyes Cárdenas

ISBN: 978-1-7338092-3-8

Published by FlowerSong Books
in the United States of America.
www.flowersongbooks.com

Set in Arial

Cover Frontexto Art: "Cruising Yanaguana" by Dr. Octavio Quintanilla
Cover design by Matthew Revert
Typeset by Matthew Revert

No part of this book may be reproduced without written permission from the publisher.

All inquiries and permission requests should be addressed to the Publisher.

PRAISE FOR TORTURED BARRIO SONGS

"Profane, profound, and poetic, this is not the standard book of poetry, but one refreshingly experimental, playfully unafraid of the power of words, and revealing a genius with the energy and brilliance of a Robin Williams, the musicality of a Beatles song, and the power of a Picasso. [Cárdenas'] … signature no-holds-barred humor, crossed with a stinging criticism of the injustices of being poor in America….a flowing and painfully beautiful novel-in-verse set in the West Side barrios of San Antonio."

—**Carmen Tafolla,**
State Poet Laureate of Texas 2015

In his heartbreaking yet hilarious poetry, rooted in a barrio that is both achingly real and hypnotically gonzo, Cárdenas explores the lives of strange, broken and marginalized men showing us the unexpected beauty and wisdom amid their unconventional lives. Like the very best of Bukowski, this Chicano Poet has spent a lifetime writing for writing's sake, because he must, porque sus dedos conocen los hechizos que hacen mágicos a los marginados.

—**David Bowles, Pura Belpré Honor-Winning author of The Smoking Mirror and They Call Me Güero: A Border Kid's Poems**

Tortured Barrio Songs will torture multi-tasking readers who won't know which to praise first. There's Reyes Cárdenas' incisive wit featuring language tricks and situational fun. There are two books under the covers, two characters singing barrio songs, readers will recognize the places. When you look underneath the funny ha-ha, there's insight, sad, lots of local color and ample satisfaction from pages of good poetry.

—**Michael Sedano, La Bloga**

In Memory Of Ruben Armando Gonzales, Jr.

CONTENTS

BOOK ONE

27	ANDRES SOBACO, EL NUMBNUTS
28	El Numbnuts Of The Westside
29	Panaderia
30	The Goodies
31	The Aztecs
32	Chihuahua
33	Garden Of Eden
34	The Rats
35	The San Antonio Creek
36	La Vida No Vale Nada
37	Mala Mujer
38	The Shooting
39	Fat Spider
40	Crickets
41	Relatives
42	Sunday Morning Coming Down
43	Borracho
44	Case Study
45	Pablito
46	Grocery Store
47	Blackbird Singing In The Dead Of Night
48	Stardust
49	Love
50	Aztec Priest
51	When Doves Cry

52	Bean And Cheese Pizza
53	The Beast
54	Cast A Giant Shadow
55	Redondo
56	The Gynecologist Of Ears
57	We Built This Country
58	Confession
59	Alias El Whatever
60	What's The Score
61	The Blessing
62	Predator
63	Cuates
64	Manco
65	Mr. Heartbreak
66	Thief
67	Siamese Cat
68	Down With Brown
69	Gentle Giant
70	S. Presa
71	Saturday Night Fever
72	Carcajada
73	Cemetery
74	Woodlawn Lake
75	Corpus Christi
76	Sgt. Pepper
77	Sins And Crimes
78	Oh Aqualung
79	What A Day For A Daydream
80	The Meaning Of Life

81	The Preacher
82	For Everything There Is A Season
83	The Westside Sun
84	Mundo Mundo
85	The Brain
86	Construction Zone
87	Uncle Baco
88	I Have A Dream
89	Lobster
90	Purse Snatcher
91	Tortured Barrio Songs
92	Uncle Pancho
93	The Bird
94	Fourth Of July
95	Milagro Central
96	Pan Dulce
97	A Day In The Life
98	The Wisdom Of Summer Rain
99	The Beginning
100	Dog Day Afternoon
101	Ladies And Gentlemen, We Have A Winner
102	Angry Westside Park
103	Dos Amigos
104	Homeless
105	Baby Sobaquito
106	For All They Were Worth
107	Asleep Inside An Old Guitar
108	Total Eclipse Of The Sun
109	A Man For All Seasons

110	Fire With Fire
111	Sir Mex A Lot
112	The Heavy Weight of America
113	Last Man On Earth
114	The Wake
115	September 11
116	Good Morning Vietnam
117	Cleaning The Beans
118	Welcome To The Jungle
119	Borrachos
120	Night Out
121	Barrio Blues
122	Grocero's Grocery Store
123	Sobaco's Barrio
124	Sobaco's Abuelo
125	Espejo
126	The Icehouse Drive Inn
127	Strangers in The Night
128	Turn On Your Love Lights, Westside
129	The Fallacy of Daiquiris
130	Into The Sunset

BOOK TWO

134	El Ocho Patas
136	Un Trip To The Outlet Mall
137	Andaba A Gatas
138	Casa Del Ocho Patas
139	El Garrapatas

140	Moon Walking Patas
141	The Young Ocho
142	Ocho Busted His Head Against His Own Head
144	Hijo Sobreviviente De La Llorona
146	Spider Vato
147	Abuela De Ocho
148	Scarecrow
150	The Roots
151	Flying Patas
152	Pata's Job
153	El Cuatro
154	The Magician's Assistant
155	The Rains Came
157	The Great Creator
159	Ocho In Love
160	Pyramid Of The Patas
161	Cumbia
162	El Ocho Vacas
164	Knew A Girl
166	El Ocho Amores
167	Mad Love
169	Ocho Clavos
170	Bouncing Benny Patas
171	His Pata Had Both Sides
173	Patas De La LLorona
174	Daddy Long Legs
176	Look Ma No Hands
177	The Musical Fruit
178	The Rescue

180	La Mosca
181	Cicada Girl
183	El Mero Mero Mero
184	Beat Poet
185	The Slave
187	Huevos Rancheros
188	Selena
190	Quetzalcoatl's Patas
192	His Obsession
194	Brown Like Me
195	El Ocho's Birthday
197	Beatle Boots
198	The Beginning Of The End

EL OCHO PATAS PART TWO

202	La Migra
203	The Golden Fleas
204	The Lynching
206	Super Ocho
207	Extra Bola
209	Star Tracalada
211	Doomsday
213	Trasero
214	I Sing The Body Electric
215	A Mother's Love
216	Sol Azteca
218	Frida Hollow
220	I Hear American Singing Its Cancion

221	Sunglasses At Night
222	The House On Manco Street
223	Amanda
225	The Big Time
226	Chicano Crash Test Dummy
227	Feet Fetish
229	Lover's Kiss
230	On The Cover Of The Rolling Stone
231	Cuates
232	Bicicleta
233	Cape Canaveral
235	Aquarena Springs
237	Otra Vez
238	Figure Eight
239	Chaleco
240	Patamerica
242	Whose Wood Was Hard
243	Sweet As A Mexican Bakery
245	Songbirds
246	Hollywood Sign
247	La Mera Mera
248	Young Love
249	La Madre
250	Son Of God
251	Arroyo
253	This Is Your Captain Speaking
255	Beauty And The Beast
256	Why Brown Boys Die
258	Some Men

259	In His Old Age
260	El Santo Canto
262	Ash Wednesday
264	Low Down
265	Inappropriate Touching
266	Estados Unidos De Vaqueros
267	He Carried Her Feet In His Feet

CANCIONES DESGRACIADAS

271	Huevos
272	Perro
273	Ranchera
274	Red Wheelbarrow
275	Howl
276	Colon
277	Aztec Lover
278	Tamales
279	Authentic Mexican Food
280	You Wanna Hear About Lupito
281	Josie
282	Teresita
283	Pedro Leos
284	The Greasy Spoon
285	Abuelo
286	Desert Cowboy
287	Salton Sea
288	Deep In The Barrio
289	I Remember Abuelo

290	Macias Bakery
291	The Mexican Boy
292	Pumpkin Empanadas
293	New Barrio Breasts
294	Fences
295	Demons
296	The Hounds Of Heaven
297	Inside A Mexican Girl
298	Hormiguero
299	Martin Street
300	Head Down
301	The Secret Of Love
302	My Chimp
303	My Seguin
304	Gallo
305	Dante
306	Toni
307	Dump Truck
308	Second Grade
309	Storm Clouds Gather

INTRODUCTION TO TORTURED BARRIO SONGS

If you have never read Reyes Cárdenas, you are probably not prepared for his unique blend of humor, wild irreverence, naked truth, and haunting philosophical depth. Profane, profound, and poetic, this is not the standard book of poetry, but one refreshingly experimental, playfully unafraid of the power of words, and revealing a genius with the energy and brilliance of a Robin Williams, the musicality of a Beatles song, and the power of a Picasso.

Tortured Barrio Songs is really not one book, but a Trinity of three books, each tied to and adding to the understanding of the others. Cárdenas brings to bear, once again, his signature no-holds-barred humor, crossed with a stinging criticism of the injustices of being poor in America, something reflected sharply in all three of the works. **Andrés Sobaco, El Numbnuts**, a flowing and painfully beautiful novel-in-verse set in the West Side barrios of San Antonio; **El Ocho Patas**, a darker, more philosophical and metaphorical tale of the man with eight legs; and **Canciones Desesperadas**, a collection of poems unveiling the formative root experiences of the poet and other real people in his Vonnegut-style karass of a barrio, together make a book both irreverent and yet somehow filled with respeto for life and the universe. The tender sacrileges with which he addresses God, or Christ, or La Llorona, remind us of a man whose tragedies have been so crushing that the hope within him has become even more persistent, and even more resilient.

In Andrés Sobaco, El Numbnuts, his work is prescient, his language rich with ambiente, with a rhythm whose beats are poetry. "His abuelo and abuela both dead/ his father and mother both dead/ death seems to run in the family Sobaco said/ his head hung sad."

We meet the obese, mean, bored-with-life desperation of El Numbnuts, a tragic anti-hero on the prowl for food and sex. He is "a fat man with fat desires." And for all the painful desperation trapping him in a life that is not what he wants it to be, these poems fill us not only with the pain of injustice but also with the ability to laugh at life with Cardenas' fine and unexpected coups of humor: " Numbnuts ….had been a carpenter just like Jesus/ but he never became a god." And "sometimes Sobaco's life/ is really death warmed over/ like refried beans / but not as good."

The reader watches, absorbed, as the heavy, hungry Sobaco, "battled the refrigerator/ in epic warfare until the cold white thing/was empty, devoid of nourishment." This is classic Reyes Cárdenas, with all objects in the universe revealing their personality in images hard to forget, like the "trash can lies on its side/ spilling its guts." He captures all of the frustration of poverty, while endowing each object or character with respect, "even the rats, prayed to their mousy God/ while gnawing on the crumbling sheetrock."

There is so much playfulness and humor in the language and the images that we begin to realize these poems are a reflection of our own lives and overlapping cultural experiences. The poem titles are Beatles songs, or conjunto classics, conversational clichés or mythic undercurrents of our lives. And the poems themselves are woven through with song lyrics, tv shows, movies, dichos, legends, nursery rhymes, advertisements, in short, all the Chicano and general American experiences of the 19th, 20th and 21st centuries. They capture the songs, the refrains, the curses and the dreams of our *gente*, all in one articulate run-on sentence of street poetry. I laughed all the way through it, and ultimately, I cried.

In **Ocho Patas** we find an even more haunting character, in a man with 8 legs, 8 heads, 8 pair of eyes. Here the poetry is profane, profound and philosophical, as in the poem *Hijo Sobreviviente De La Llorona*, where "El ocho patas/ lived in the past/ and he lived/ in the future/ the present/ was only temporary." El Ocho Patas takes us even further out in the universe, though always based back in the barrio. In clever and bold language play, unafraid of word boundaries, Cárdenas takes us between dimensions of the historic, the folkloric, the celestial, and the mundane, tell-it-like-it-is barrio. In this book, you are as likely to encounter the Aztecs as The Twilight Zone, and La Llorona as Dos Tetas Park. You will be shocked, maybe scandalized, at how they act, but Cárdenas keeps us focused on the big picture, even in the tiny details. We are asked to consider it from a perspective of "all of antkind" and then brought back to humility "...because you pendejo that you are/ were made of stardust/ common everyday lousy stardust."

Rasquache style, but with haunting and symbolic images, he takes clichés and turns them into "found art." Simple street language carries additional layers of meaning here, where everything has its humor, its tragedy, its cruelty, and its hope. We watch Ocho Patas go from a baby to an adaptable crawling teenager, a lover, a villain, a reflection of ourselves, and we even see him express himself as God, Jesus, La Llorona, a millipede, a country....

And just as we think we understand where this book is going, Cardenas takes us to the most painful and most contradictory of all the three—the

Canciones Desesperadas—where he lays bare the poems of his own life and the lives of those around him, in a confessional of pain, lust, hunger, and survival.

This book, is a mind-bending escapade into reality in all its infinite dimensions. It is not pretty, it is not correct. It does not follow the agreed-upon conventions. It crashes the convention with blood, sweat, and human excrement. Experimental and honest, it is the voice of a true poet, who will make you laugh and cry and question and end up with *respeto* for the misfits and the mice, the barrio dogs and the borrachines, the young girls murdered at the park, and everyone who ever hopes to undergo growth, understanding, or transformation, like El Numbnuts, who "suddenly/ steps out of his fat body/ and blossoms like bull nettle."

Carmen Tafolla,
State Poet Laureate of Texas 2015

This is the day of the expanding man.

from Deacon Blues
by Steely Dan

BOOK ONE

ANDRES SOBACO, EL NUMBNUTS

Andres Sobaco nicknamed el Numbnuts
by the kids in his junior high school because
of his numbskull behavior and all-around stupidity
grew up to be an adult form of his junior high self.
In this incarnation, el Numbnuts is a heavy-set Chicano
living in the Westside of San Antonio, in a house
which belonged to his abuela, his grandmother,
who lived long, long ago, in a galaxy far, far away.

EL NUMBNUTS OF THE WESTSIDE

El Numbnuts was obese had bad knees
was nothing to sneeze at
otherwise he was unhealthy
a bad to the bone mojon
he had a way with words
that made you hurt
but he also had a soft side
his nalgas were flabby as hell
Numbnuts lived
in the baddest barrio of them all
the mean streets of the Westside
where a look could get you killed
where no one had abuelas anymore
where the weak peed
when the strong decreed
but nobody ever messed with Sobaco

PANADERIA

El Numbnuts was a favorite customer
at la panaderia Las Panzonas on the corner
of San Luis Street y Caquitas Street
buying up all the empanadas y marranitos
his tattoo of Jesus proudly on his forearm
he was wearing a yellow wife-beater
it used to be white once
the barrio kids made fun of him
but only behind his back
you know like most people
El Numbnuts got behind the wheel
of his 1958 Chevy
the one with the rounded fins
a contradiction of the age
he pulled into his gravel driveway
and honked to make the chickens move
the mangy dog growled
and El Numbnuts
kicked at him affectionately
pinche gordo the dog said under its breath

THE GOODIES

El Numbnuts munched on the goodies
he had bought at the bakery
while he drank a beer
and watched porno
on his Windows 3.1 computer
the neighbors were fighting again
like all good neighbors do
the teenage girl pregnant at 13
the son sold crack
to the ten year olds down the street
the smelly city bus
black as a caterpillar
climbed the bridge
over the railroad tracks
its prickly hair stung like cactus
El Numbnuts farted into the sofa
stretched and volunteered

THE AZTECS

In his youth El Numbnuts
had been a carpenter just like Jesus
but he never became a god
instead he had turned into this
a fat guy who lived in the barrio
the barrio didn't know
the barrio was a burro
like all barrios
hee-hawing next to the taco stand
annoying the Sunday morning customers
looking for barbacoa
to cure their hangovers
El Numbnuts had a hangover too
bigger than the Pyramid of the Sun
his head felt just as heavy
he cursed the damn Aztecs
and the Aztecs
with a pissed off look on their faces
wondered what the hell did we do

CHIHUAHUA

All the barrio bitches were in heat
El Numbnuts' perro sported a grin
from ear to ear to ear
a deformity that endeared him
to his fat master
who just now was snoring
on the poor sofa
which groaned in pain
having to support the weight
of such an ass day after day
sit on the recliner please
the sofa begged in sofa language
but el Numbnuts had no clue
and the perro was quite busy
impregnating a Chihuahua in the alley

GARDEN OF EDEN

El Numbnut's backyard was small and trashy

nothing like the Garden of Eden

more like a desert

it hadn't been so when his abuela

was still alive and kicking

she had always pushed her grandson

to better himself and he tried

but the barrio has a way

of bringing you back down

to its own level sooner or later

and the front porch was no better

with its view of the downtown skyscrapers

including the Tower which protruded like a verga

screwing up his worthless aspirations

THE RATS

The rats that lived in El Numbnut's casa
often talked about their landlord
calling him a fat lazy glutton
the ungrateful little vermin
didn't let a day go by
without insulting the gordo
warm and cozy in the walls
they lay on their backs
stretched their legs
and flicked their tails
while Numbnuts
battled the refrigerator
in epic warfare
until the cold white thing
was empty devoid of nourishment
the worried rats peered from the porch
as el Numbnuts drove off
to the Michoacana Supermercado
or maybe just to the 7-11
the rats prayed to their mousy God
while gnawing on the crumbling sheetrock

THE SAN ANTONIO CREEK

El Numbnuts was sweating up a storm
at the conjunto festival
Dos Tetas Park was full
of accordion aficionados
pickpockets a few whores
and goddamn children
running around eating raspas
old men drinking beer
or their own spit
if they had any left
after living such a long life
el Numbnuts stared at the babes
chicas in short shorts
his verga undecided
about this chiquita or that
his banana had dark black spots
Santiago the Cricket famous cabron
was playing Viva Seguin
el Numbnut's khaki pants
were soaked in sweat
and as he stood up
he flooded the San Antonio Creek
sweeping away the Westside trash
and maybe a pinche pato or two

LA VIDA NO VALE NADA

Over my head said el Numbnuts
the clouds drag their asses south
in the alley a trash can
lies on its side spilling its guts
in the distance the downtown buildings
sway in the sunlight
to my right
between two abandoned houses
dog shit becomes coal then diamonds
I lean back in my chair on the porch
as the Westside darkens
I have wasted my life

MALA MUJER

El Numbnuts goes for a Sunday drive
out on Texas 16 way beyond
where Angela de Hoyos lived
where only her widower Sandy lives now
long hair and dark clothes
Numbnuts stops his car along a barbed wire fence
a pony strolls up to him
its mane fluttering
like a butterfly in the breeze
its ear pulls away from his hand
like a brown girl turned off
suddenly el Numbnuts
steps out of his fat body
and blossoms like bull nettle

THE SHOOTING

El Numbnut's neighbors were shot dead
mother and son and other
neighboring houses were shot at too
the barrio is boiling in the cold
icebergs crash into the bakery
conchas shiver in glass cases
polar bears float by in rubber dingys
el Numbnuts paces on his porch
the police swarm the street
in blue parkas and bulletproof bullets ricochet
the barrio is a barrio is a barrio
Numbnuts steps back inside
the sofa cringes the flat screen screams
all is right with the world

FAT SPIDER

La Virgen de Guadalupe is a fat spider
in el Numbnuts closet
where clothes have been hanging
since the early 90's
stale as bread and moldy green
his favorite color
the t-shirts of the era
scream for attention and get none
La Virgen patiently waits for flies
or roaches or other spiders
La Virgen is a cannibal if need be
el Numbnuts is drinking beer
the beer squirming on the way down
praying and whispering God help me
but God has abandoned this part of the barrio
and La Virgen ignores our tangled webs
oh ye of little faith

CRICKETS

The crickets had taken over the street
in front of el Numbnut's house
occasionally a car went by
and crushed them like peanuts
their shells littered San Luis Street
a leg or two discernable
autumn hung in the air
from its Westside swing
its chains rusty and noisy
a Catholic school girl
put down her backpack
ran to the slide
and slid out of sight for the moment
a cricket jumped on the merry-go-round
pretending to be at ease
its mind policed by dark juices
el Numbnuts yawned at life
.

RELATIVES

How it came about that
La Llorona's relatives
ended up moving in with el Numbnuts
we will not soon know
only that they had a proclivity
for trying to drown their own children
and how those children
managed to grow up
is another mystery
but el Numbnuts was a gracious host
and never complained about his guests
who always wandered off
to the San Antonio arroyo
held their kids in front of them and you could swear
they were going to shove them
into the dirty nasty arroyo

SUNDAY MORNING COMING DOWN

Eating cottage cheese right out
of its container while outside
the trees are real trees
and a blade of grass
cast out by the others
refuses to sway in the breeze
lackluster affair of this Sunday morning
el Numbnuts in khaki pants
gray shirt and open eyes for once
nearby a converted storefront
turned church attracts
no one's attention not even God's
his angels gamble in the fire
earwax builds up slowly
in Sobaco's fat ears
Rome wasn't built in a day

BORRACHO

In the barrio the sun always comes up
wearing a sombrero
talking English with a Mexican accent
smelling of breakfast tacos
a serape wrapped around his shoulders
while his wife the moon
in old worn chanclas
shuffles around in what's left
of the sky not fouled by man
and our hero Sobaco el Numbnuts
lets out a fart
full of last night's beer
and laments that the woman
he tried to pick up last night
at Benny's Westside watering charco
wakes up in another man's arms
just blocks away
her panties have replaced the American flag

CASE STUDY

Overheard by el Numbnut's

gigantically obese earlobes

a mother telling her 11 year old daughter

pull those shorts

out of your butt and camel toe

imagine if you will

Rod Serling claiming

that this happened in the Twilight Zone

in black and white

back in the 1950's

but our fat friend says nah

I heard it with my own ears

the things dumb blondes will say

he said to his beer belly

his navel among the missing

PABLITO

You people do not know me
my name is Pablito
I am el Numbnut's dog
or so the fat slob assumes
my opinion of people
is worse than my bite
and contrary to popular opinion
I do not enjoy
smelling other dog's asses
it runs in my family I guess
we can talk more later
but right now I am going to try
to get that gordo to fill my bowl
with that imitation bacon crap
which I'm supposed to love so much
according to that tub of lard
sitting over there scratching himself

GROCERY STORE

Andres Sobaco was a fat man with fat man desires
at the grocery store
he eyed girls as if they were food
skinny tortilla type girls
big girls whose lust for tamales
matched his own appetite
he pushed the cart
as if he was pushing
on a big girl's ass
he thumped on watermelons
smiled and thought to himself
ah a woman's breasts this hard
would be tough to sleep on
his mind worked in mysterious ways
or his mind did not work at all
at the checkout counter he asked the cashier
"How much for the women?"
the customers in line behind him
do not get it and they never will
the cashier's blank face says it all
the human race
has survived despite itself

BLACKBIRD SINGING IN THE DEAD OF NIGHT

What would happen if Andres Sobaco
el Numbnuts was a black bird
stuck in the barrio like the rest of us
eating pebbles and forsaking
dragonflies and earthworms
after a dirty barrio rain
you know the kind of rain
I'm talking about
oily and hanging over the streets
that haven't been repaved since 1960
and Sobaco flaps his dark dark wings
you'd think night had descended
out of nowhere and caught you
by surprise indisposed indiscreet
cheating on your wife
with your wife's underage niece
just then Andres the black bird flies off
to the neighbor's rotting chinaberry tree
you see him arching his back to poop

STARDUST

Andres el Numbnuts was not made from stardust
no cabrones he was made from
the pure emptiness of space
his eyes were made from anti-space
his heart was made from
the hardened droppings of empty space
that's why when you run into him
at the bakery or at the gas station
you stare at him and say
what the hell is wrong with that vato
what the hell is wrong with that dude
but you can't put your finger on it
because you pendejo that you are
were made of stardust
common everyday lousy stardust

LOVE

El Numbnuts had once loved a girl so much
that he wore her out literally wore her out
rubbed the flesh right off of her with his flecha
wore out her beautiful lips with besos
wore down her heart until
it was only a few hollow veins
wore down her butt
until only the tailbone was left
wore out her arms
until the bones became windchimes
even the wind exclaimed
"What up here!"
el Numbnuts had once loved a girl
so goddamn much that he wore her out
nothing left of her nothing at all
now that's what I call love

AZTEC PRIEST

Sobaco, fat ass that he was
had heart problems of course
he didn't have insurance
which is the American way
so he crossed Trump's fence into Mexico
found an Aztec priest in Tepito
the priest cut out Sobaco's heart
tinkered with it
like only an Aztec priest knows how
and Sobaco's heart was as good as new
our fat ass Sobaco alias el Numbnuts
came back to the States running
though he'd never been able to run before
his woman-like breasts bouncing up and down
goddamn Mexican making America great again

WHEN DOVES CRY

When doves cry our fat Andres Sobaco
comes out to his porch with his BB gun
and starts shooting at the flock of beasts
the rotund mound of no rebound
hates doves and other flying animals
we're sure he'd shoot pterodactyls
if they sat on his telephone wires
sagging them like musical notes
Jesus, it's really awful
when he comes out in his muscle shirt
sits in his car with the door open
blaring his radio to Teddy Trunk
and His Tapados early Sixties stuff
and the fat slob
can't even cripple one damn dove
at least he gives peace a chance

BEAN AND CHEESE PIZZA

Andres Sobaco's favorite pizza
was bean and cheese pizza
made by his abuela
because gringos didn't know how to make it
back in the day God bless her soul
fried bean and cheese pizza to die for
and of course it had its side effects
look at Sobaco's panza
that ain't all beer in there amigo
abuela you oughta open a franchise
he tells his grandmother
who tells him tas loco mijo
and as the big fat ass folds
a bean and cheese slice of pizza
his eyes roll into the back of his head
like those of a great white shark
when he bites off the arm
of a nice young white girl
just beyond the breakers

THE BEAST

" He who makes a beast of himself
gets rid of the pain of being a man."
                                   Doctor Johnson

Normally el Numbnuts was just
like any ordinary fat ass
nothing special to see here move along
but once in awhile not too often thank God
but every once in awhile
the fat ass would turn into a beast
who would satisfy his animal desires
at whatever cost it cost
in those wild moments
the female form was merely an object
a receptacle a place to plunge into
the seed was not important
just the planting of it
whether the ground was fertile or not
did not matter at all
and after the monstrous fire
had been put out
he became just the average fat ass again
which seems about right in our eyes

CAST A GIANT SHADOW

Sobaco's shadow is big and round
if the sun tries to peek around it it can't
if an ant walks into Sobaco's shadow
it scares the bejeebers out of it
forgets to follow the scent of his brother
forgets it can lift
ten times its own weight
poops right there in public
have you ever seen ant shit
it would surprise you
how big their turds are
so when Sobaco walks under a tree
and stops casting shadows
we and all of antkind are indebted to him

REDONDO

Sobaco's pet bird had been born
with just one wing
he flew around in circles
in the living room
and when Sobaco took his bird
out on the front porch
Sobaco didn't worry
about the bird flying away
Sobaco had named the bird Redondo
which meant round in English
for all of you who are Spanishly challenged
Sobaco would laugh his butt off
when Redondo bounced off shit
and looked forlorn as other birds
flew by laughing at him
human or fowl we're all assholes

THE GYNECOLOGIST OF EARS

Andres Sobaco could always tell
if a girl was in heat
by just tasting her earwax
rolling it around in his mouth
and spitting out the watery wax
into the palm of his hand
almost like a goddamn curandero
meanwhile the girl is hot as hell
her panties all excited
and el Numbnuts
is judging earwax
assuring that his diagnoses
is irrefutable
the son of a bitch is good
he knows women inside and out
is that why they hate him?

WE BUILT THIS COUNTRY

We built this country said Andres Sobaco
as he piddled around on the streets
of the Westside
where the sound of the freeway
smelled like gringo tacos
from Taco Belle
which had recently burnt down thank God
and the black puddles of yesterday's rain
reflected Sobaco's face
it intrigued Sobaco for a second
but he persevered
yes we built this country
from its buildings to its bridges
to its highways even to its very jails
where they confine us
but we built this country
like it or not
Sobaco had never lifted a hand

CONFESSION

The fantasies of el gordo cannot be ignored
he lusted after the grandmother and the granddaughter
who lived two houses down on Chaveta Street
he spied on them with binoculars
whenever they walked by his house
on their way to the barrio grocery store
Don Lalo had owned the store
since before dinosaurs walked the earth
or so it seemed
and not even the arrival
of the new superstores
could put him out of business
the granddaughter was voluptuous
the grandmother didn't seem to age
el gordo's lust was as big as his stomach
when he went to confession
he told the priest of his sin
and the priest said yes I know her granddaughter
el gordo heard the priest sigh like an angel

ALIAS EL WHATEVER

Andres Sobaco alias El Whatever
was listening to Bennie Y Las Jetas
on a rainy day on the Westside
remembering things he'd done and said
love was a puddle in the street
which fathered punks and cabrones and ladrones
and young girls up to no good
Sobaco had seen it all
and he had seen nothing
he was an innocent babe
and he was guilty as hell
a nun had once pulled his ear off
that's why he can't hear
music had rotted the wooden floors
of the house his abuelo had built
the house abuela left
to her favorite grandson
Andres Sobaco both vaca and man
our very own sacred cow

WHAT'S THE SCORE

With young blue eyes she tells
our fat friend to get off her thigh
little else must be said
one of Sobaco's rare scores
the law can't check the crime scene
if there's no witnesses
a dog barks outside the window
not Redondo's imitations but another mutt
Sobaco gets into his boxer shorts
she slides into her leggings
puts her bra into her coat pocket
the sun is just setting itself up
a car or two drag their feet
on the ancient asphalt out front
remnants of a sidewalk
surface like a snake head in the creek
and Sobaco's manhood
sports the girl's DNA

THE BLESSING

A Thievery of James Wright

El gordo once made love to a fat girl
pulling her big thighs apart
his mind lingered on her soft flesh
the tuft of hair surrounding her vagina
wondering if God had really made this shit up
as he inches forward
the fat girl's breathing
building up inside her breasts
which were surprisingly small
her pink nipples like yellow roses
they both moaned as the bed creaked
somewhere nearby a dog barked
against its rusty chain
its water bowl empty and overturned
suddenly el gordo realized
that if he stepped out of his fat body right now
he'd break into an ugly greasy blossom

PREDATOR

Andres Sobaco alias el Numbnuts panzon
became a predator at a tender young age
he preyed on candy and cookies and soda
anything sweet he molested
he fondled he caressed
he took advantage of
there was no cure for his illness
no sweets were safe from him
even if those sweets
belonged to relatives or friends
he preyed on Girl Scout cookies
he couldn't stay out of bakeries
that's him here with cake crumbs
on his pimpled face
in his high school yearbook

CUATES

And so Andres was two men at once
the man he portrayed himself to be
and the man only he himself knew
the self that would disgust
and the self he accepted
in that he was no different than you
though you might argue
though you might want to cry and kick
Andres Sobaco only dealt with the truth
if he molested some young girl
if he killed a black man out of hate
if he ran over a housewife
and left the scene with a dented fender
that was Sobaco pure as a baby
and just as innocent he thought
as he became one with himself

MANCO

Sobaco in the cantina stares hard
at a vieja's ass until his eyes
made of glass begin to fog up
conjunto music blares away
in Sobaco's deaf ears
ears full of wax living in there for years
Andres Sobaco is like a moco
in the nose of the barrio
which will not go away
no matter what the rich
do or say no way
Sobaco sits at the bar
and then goes home
to his loneliness and limp

MR. HEARTBREAK

Mr. Heartbreak alias el Numbnuts Sobaco
was trimming his toenails with pliers
because they were thick with fungus
while admiring his birdbaths
which had become his sole obsession
birds in the barrio you ask
yes we have birds in the barrio
Mr. Heartbreak was thinking
of the girl he loved
even though she did not love him back
his heartbeat like a rubberband
old and brittle
it could snap at any moment
a neighbor's rooster stood in a tree
its redness like the sun
the sky his cape
Andres Sobaco sighed
daydreaming little bubbles of love
the bubbles popped by sharp barrio dust

THIEF

Sobaco was on the run from the law
he had stolen someone's thunder
and damn if he was gonna give it back
in the far reaches of the Westside
he sought refuge behind
an abandoned cantina and dry cleaners
he munched on a bag of Fritos
a cop car cruised by
a city bus polluted Cabrona Street
the passengers were losers like him
thought Sobaco as he examined
the stolen thunder for the first time
I wonder how much
this will get me at the pawn shop
it looked like it might rain
goddamn pinche clouds
this morning the weather girl had said no

SIAMESE CAT

Once when Andres Sobaco was twenty-three
he killed a Siamese cat
and waited patiently for its twin to appear
it never showed
plunging Sobaco
in the study of pseudo-science
which at his advanced age
he has finally mastered
he won't get fooled again
he don't believe in false gods
he don't believe in sacred cows
he eats hamburgers as well as tacos
he don't believe in black cats
or white men
he don't believe in miracles
he don't believe that things
happen for a reason
he don't believe in fate
he don't believe that love
is the cure for hate
he's a well-rounded individual
as his belly will prove

DOWN WITH BROWN

Sobaco was down with brown
more than you think fink
Sobaco had always been
all about dem beans
he kept quiet about it
no use to scream
he fought long and hard
even though it was useless
down at Centeno
he bought veneno
up at the mall
he peed in the restroom stall
on the Westside
he sat on his porch
or observed the barrio
from his beat up carro
he was no ordinary charro
but his feet were made of clay
until this very day

GENTLE GIANT

On the outside Sobaco seemed
like a normal human being
on the inside huge boulders
blocked the way
weeds grew viciously
wild rivers spit in your face
dogs mauled little girls
at Centeno Supermarket
Sobaco looked normal
as he pushed the grocery cart
around the aisles and parking lot
but on the inside
Sobaco broke out of prison
killed a female guard
forest fires raged on his face
his hands choked back tears
women were minced meat
on the outside
Sobaco was a gentle giant
as he tried to start his car

S. PRESA

Andres Sobaco alias el Numbnuts
tries to pick up a girl on S. Presa
trying to impresa
he revs the engine
it misses and backfires
darn the bad luck
he drives to the 7-11
buys a cold drink and Redskin peanuts
heads back to the Westside
where the sun festers
and dogs nudge its round ball of fire
where the boys are a goldmine of shit
that barrio girls sniff
Sobaco pulls into his driveway
which is falling apart like his heart

SATURDAY NIGHT FEVER

Tonight the Westside is as happy as a rat
its whiskers bouncing its tail slapping
eyes brighter that the moon
a stray dog bounces like a marble
off silver trash cans
in the gold-colored alley
tonight men and women
don't even need sex to feel alive
Andres Sobaco sits in his car
listening to the radio
and the driveway sinks it teeth
into Sobaco's windy behind
meanwhile Sobaco longs
for the neighbor's granddaughter
who just now is opening curtains
in a t-shirt made of flesh
soon it will be Sunday even for God's nuts

CARCAJADA

The more he thought about America
the more he laughed
its great expanse without pants
its heart in the wrong place
its balls dragging
on the purple mountain majesties
its founding fathers floundering
Andres Sobaco laughed to himself
as he sat on his porch
the Westside was a pot of gold
at the end of a brown rainbow
that used to be the American Dream
before Miss Liberty got come upon

CEMETERY

At the cemetery Andres Sobaco
sweaty armpits and all
stood by his mother's grave
who he had lost when
he was only twelve years old
of course he remembers her vividly
but he can't remember
a single word they exchanged
his mother in a sunbonnet
walking between rows of tall corn
his mother washing clothes
in an old washing machine
with the old-fashioned wringers
his mother drawing well water
with a bucket in the backyard
feeding the goat or the calf
and now she lies here
in this meaningless goddamn grave
Sobaco curses God's useless ass

WOODLAWN LAKE

Years ago parked at Woodlawn Lake
Sobaco remembered the girl
who drowned herself because of love
and still haunts the lake
to this very day
Sobaco was heartbroken
when they pulled her body out
her arms stiff as the freeway
quiet as a cathedral
lips which could tell no lie
Sobaco ws drinking a Hippo soda water
that had lost its taste
like the girl's thighs no doubt
and when he turned on the car to leave
the engine noise
was like a shadow the sun
could not brighten
Sobaco's heart pumped blood
in all directions as he drove off

CORPUS CHRISTI

His abuelo and abuela both dead
his father and mother both dead
death seems to run in the family Sobaco said
his head hung sad
but such is life he thought with a smile
as he threw some clothes
into the back seat of the car
he was taking a short vacation
going to Corpus Christi
and check out the babes in bikinis
bikini was just a fancy name for panties
it's all a state of mind
drinking beer as he drove south
the landscape changed little
abandoned tiny towns cropped up
and as suddenly were gone
just like abuela Fernanda's
delicious square bean tamales
and then the salt air
shook Sobaco back to reality

SGT. PEPPER

Sobaco looked like the Maharishi Yogi
but all screwed up inside
couldn't help the Beatles at all
but ogled their girlfriends
Come Together is not after all
one of his pet peeves
so Sobaco fends for himself
sins pre-sins post-sins
the man has no qualms
about anything really
if only he wore his Sgt. Pepper suit
at least we'd be warned
of what the hell
was going on in his head
but living in the barrio
is a good disguise

SINS AND CRIMES

For his past sins and crimes
he atoned by committing more crimes
but on this humid San Antonio morning
he rode the bus downtown
since his car wasn't running
insisted on backfiring instead
and trembling like a puppy
but Sobaco had business to attend to
at the tax office
where the girls wore perfume
if only to pleasure
he paid with a check
the property taxes
so damn overprized
for the shack he lived in
the Westside over-valued
and over praised
by those who lived there
if only out of spite

OH AQUALUNG

Girls drove him mad
unripe girls at the park
in a hurry to grow up
Sobaco's armpits like a lake
summer trees hid
in their own trunks from the heat
squirrels swam in empty fountains
the Westside was hot as hell
the devil climbed into a refrigerator
which lay on its side
Sobaco's sweaty ass
sat in his car
Sobaco escaped to the mall sometimes
where his soul was cleansed
of everything wrong with America
or so he thought

WHAT A DAY FOR A DAYDREAM

Sobaco had no real friends
imaginary or not
made up or made down
life is always lived sideways
sometimes in the past
sometimes in the future
sure Sobaco daydreamed
who doesn't
some things he daydreamed
were against the law
some things he daydreamed
seemed cruel and unusual punishment
the past was sordid
and the future iffy
Sobaco lay in bed like melted ice cream

THE MEANING OF LIFE

One fine day Andres Sobaco
alias el Numbnuts
held the sun in his hands
rolled it around in his palms
like a marble from his childhood
on the gravel schoolyard
fat ugly duckling
that everyone said he would outgrow
but alas no such thing
came to pass
and here standing before you
is the fat ass Sobaco
still accomplishing nothing
but life is not about that
life is not meant to be special
Sobaco smiles

THE PREACHER

Andres Sobaco walked towards
the pitiful barrio sunset
like a gunfighter
or maybe like Winnie the Pooh
who knows anything
in this day and age
Sobaco pondered his past
trying to change it
because he knew
he couldn't change the future
the future being set in stone
the future which knows us
all too well
and will punish us all
like a vengeful God
though there be none
and therein lies the caca
which Sobaco had always preached
if he preached anything at all

FOR EVERYTHING THERE IS A SEASON

Sobaco sweat and shit
didn't give a damn about English Lit
he swayed to the Westside wind
he stood still for the calm
the sun was square
when the moon was not there
once during one of those
very rare Westside snows
when there was no nose to blows
Sobaco put on his coat
left footprints in the snow
made snow angels on Zarzamora Street
shook off the frostbite from his feet
remembered when women were sweet
in an hour it will be summer
that's how life treated Sobaco

THE WESTSIDE SUN

The Westside sun can suck
the blood and guts out of you
whether you stand or struggle
Sobaco was a big man
he kicked and screamed
the neighbors said
what the hell?
but otherwise he stayed put
the curtains were more
that you could taste
or spit out
the city bus laid clouds of dust
on the neighbor's roses
and the thorns said
come here come here
Sobaco dealt with adversity
so well
but it's not for us to say
his sweaty armpits hold sway
that's all that's all

MUNDO MUNDO

The wonders of the world
seemed to have passed Sobaco by
and Sobaco never even batted
one of his fat-assed eyebrows
and though beauty was more than nalgas
you couldn't tell him that
at the dance he was always looking
for the devil with rooster feet
instead of the cumbia beat
el panzon sucked down a beer
thinking that failure was near
he asked a girl to dance
and she said eww
so he cumbia'd by himself
his sweaty armpits rubbed against the world
and the world curled up into a ball

THE BRAIN

Chew on Sobaco's brain if you wish
feel the lobes the bumps the lumps
that doctors will say are quite odd
the hard veins neurons out of place
the medulla oblongata
crawling along like a gata
female cat for those of you
non-Spanish speakers
bounce his brain on the floor if you wish
like a football it will bounce
in crazy ways
which can't be predicted
Sobaco's fat brain will float
like a water spider
like a gondola or speedboat
Sobaco's brain would make a great soup
if we were cannibals
oh wait we are

CONSTRUCTION ZONE

Obsessed as he is with the girl
his arms are awful jets
his stomach a rotting wooden fence
his heart a rotary phone
beige as the day he was born
he kidnaps her sweet little feet
ravishes boulders in the ravine
asphalt flies in his pockets
"oh these jets I hold her down with
my tongue a butcher knife
the fine cuts no one sees
or bothers to fold up…"
obsessed as he was
with her hot little body
he broke like a piece of glass
that had already broken once
follow his trail if you dare
the orange cones are there

UNCLE BACO

" No, Uncle Baco, the name of the show

was not Secret Asian Man."

says his niece to Sobaco

who's talking about a 1960's tv show

his niece googled to find out

what her uncle was talking about

meanwhile Sobaco considered the Internet

a corruption of knowledge

a tool that had driven society apart

a disease which had spread

around the world

sucking the blood out of reality

and just as quickly Sobaco

dropped the subject

went to the refrigerator for a beer

and swore that life was good

I HAVE A DREAM

Sobaco's dream is dragged through
the dirty streets of the Westside
gathering dirt and grime like a snowball
brown as hell by the time
it gets to Mi Tierra
where the marranitos beckon
and the girls in shorts
show off lemon slices
Sobaco always thought
there'd be a light at the end of the tunnel
but not the drop off
pendejo ain't got a bit of sense
like most of us I guess
yet as long as the wind
pushes the stars against his collar
Sobaco will go on dreaming

LOBSTER

Like a lobster dropped into a pot
of boiling water
Sobaco screamed in pain
but nobody heard him
he could see the bubbling water
at the top of the pot
felt hot and hotter
he could not hear himself
scream anymore
he wondered if he was dead
he felt them tearing his limbs apart
digging into the shells of his arms
digging the flesh out of his tail
his eyes popped out
but nobody saw
his whiskers twitched one last time
and lay on the plate
after everybody ate

PURSE SNATCHER

Sobaco once tried to make
a living as a petty thief
hung around in the Westside grocery store parking lots
snatched purses from old ladies
but his fat ass ran a few steps
and he collapsed to the ground
out of breath and sweating
like the San Antonio River
sometimes the old ladies giggled at him
sometimes they threw him a dollar or two
but they never called the cops
bystanders just scratched their heads
and went about their business
sometimes a life of crime
doesn't even get you time

TORTURED BARRIO SONGS

Sobaco's barrio tortured as it is

is still full of songs

hurtful songs sweet songs

songs down on their luck

songs which rise above everything else

songs which drag us under

Sobaco's always level-headed

in his struggles

somehow managing

to never win or lose

that's the magic of the Westside

its songs without words

and its words without song

tortured barrio songs

that live on and on

UNCLE PANCHO

Stars are the greasy little wheels
that power child molestation said Sobaco
to no one in particular
and of course to everyone in particular
Sobaco had been molested
by his Uncle Pancho
in his grandfather's barn
on an old buggy
Sobaco still remembers
the hard dusty leather seats
and the hay wafting about
in the dim sunlight
sunlight that came in
through the barn doors
his backside hurt
but his Uncle's moaning
worried Sobaco more
wondering what pain
he himself had inflicted
on his poor Uncle Pancho

THE BIRD

Andres Sobaco woke up in the morning

and he was a black bird

he thought oh well

at least I'll be able to fly

he swooped up

to the nearest tree

almost lost his balance

down below the barrio

busted a move

while Sobaco shook his tail feathers

and splattered

a swing set down below

the breakfast worm

was no breakfast taco he thought

he drank water from a muddy puddle

on Zarzamora Street

it tasted like instant coffee

Sobaco spent the day

flying here and there

and his little bird brain

was able to muster up a sarcastic thought

this flying crap

ain't all it's cracked up to be

and he lost his balance once again

FOURTH OF JULY

Andres Sobaco celebrating the Fourth of July
on the Westside of San Antonio
where bullets fly out of the American flag
which betrays him and the other Westsiders
but Sobaco barbecues his tacos
and drinks his beer
listens to the Star-Spangled Banner
played by Jimi Hendrix
or by El Parche
and Sobaco realizes that the past is gone
and the future
belongs to the white man
yet Sobaco is an optimist
about his pessimism
and he celebrates the Fourth
for what it ain't
and for what it will never be

MILAGRO CENTRAL

Miracles still happen on the dirty Westside

Sobaco gets laid by a loose girl

the Hemisfair Tower towers

the San Antonio River

breathes like a fish

an oily bubble surfaces for air

the Mexican bakeries

ramp up production

concha after concha

is shoved up our bocas locas

the old greasy asphalt

burns the feet of stray dogs

who bark louder than the Lord himself

the girl's scent lies on Sobaco's bed for days

Sobaco's fat belly rises up and down like Lazarus

never underestimate the Westside

PAN DULCE

Sobaco's dream girl walks by the front
of his dilapidated house
rare as a unicorn
her blue jean cut offs
match the movement of the barrio
stride for stride
the sweetness of it bubbling up
like the old San Pedro Springs
before man corrupted them
Sobaco's dream girl
her chest moving up and down
pulled up by the moon and sun
and down by the gravity of earth
at this moment this bitter barrio
is sweeter than the insides
of a Mexican bakery

A DAY IN THE LIFE

A dragonfly stabbed at a pool of water
Sobaco had left the water hose on
the dragonfly darted back and forth
as it stabbed the puddle with his knife
Sobaco thought what a way
to drink water
Sobaco's life darted back and forth too
though he himself didn't realize it
he didn't realize anything really
he sat on the porch
as a city bus defecated on the street
the wind blew in square pieces
and round pieces
and the hot sky cracked open
Sobaco's sweaty shorts
stuck to his nalgas
like a pretty girl
sticks to a cute boy
at the carnival

THE WISDOM OF SUMMER RAIN

The summer storm rolled into the Westside
with black clouds and slow lightning
the wind blew in the trees
like an old maricon
the rain pleased the young lesbian neighbor
who pretended to live
Sobaco sat on his rickety porch
enjoying the small hail
as it bounced off his knuckles
his abuela had loved
this kind of storms
though she'd rush
to cover all the mirrors in the house
abuela's slight bones
probably all that remained of her
and the strong brave hair
the thunder startled Sobaco's dog Pablito
whose mind wandered in and out of the future
Sobaco picked his nose
as the storm quietly moved on
to the Northwest Side
to kill some ignorant motorist
who'd driven into a low water crossing
Sobaco applauded what little justice
was left in the world

THE BEGINNING

Overgrown with weeds, Sobaco's yard
often rolled its eyes as the fat man
pulled a weed or two and then gave up
the yard would giggle
and a stone or two would shake
their hard heads against the sky
inside the rundown house
the sink drowned with dishes
the soapy water
had long ago lost its personality
a chair lay askew on the kitchen floor
the radio was tuned to KCOR
for whatever ungodly reason
out the kitchen window
a neighbor could be seen
maybe still alive
hanging clothes on a leaning clothesline
the wind skirted the clothes
how will they ever dry
thought a sickly sparrow
Sobaco rattled inside the house
cigarette smoke floated like the moon
and a dirty rolled up carpet
had just begun

DOG DAY AFTERNOON

In a moment of weakness
Sobaco had once let the widow Lomas
seduce him one hot afternoon
as she opened her dark brown thighs
the veins and stretch marks scared him
but not his brainless manhood
her lips hung like windchimes
the moans she made
stung Sobaco deep in his chest
the bed kicked like a jackass
every which way but loose
the widow Lomas lay like a puddle
left by a hot rain
soon an oily film rose to the top
Sobaco's sweat soaked the sheets
that would never dry again
until the Amazon forest
was chopped down for good
the widow Lomas dressed
and smiled like the sun
Sobaco slinked home to shower
his dog lowered its head and tail
to no avail

LADIES AND GENTLEMEN, WE HAVE A WINNER

Sometimes Sobaco's life

is a brand new penny

Lincoln happy as hell to be alive

the Confederate States vanquished

Robert E. Lee the color of pee

sometimes Sobaco's life

is not worth a plugged nickel

Washington's wooden teeth

full of termites

the British gloating

over their victory

sometimes Sobaco's life

is really death warmed over

like refried beans

but not as good

ANGRY WESTSIDE PARK

Andres Sobaco el Numbnuts at the park
his fat ass barely fits on the swing
the park is dirty like every Westside park
the dirt is ancient and the water fountains
last worked during the Kennedy Administration
a city bus grunts like a marrano
as it picks up Mexicans with blank faces
Sobaco eyes the slide and the seesaw
way out of his league
a soft wind swirls like a stick
the clouds stand out like a bugger
on a pretty girl's nose
Sobaco walks home with a limp
note to self
don't jump off the swing again
when he gets home he opens a beer
gotta get hydrated
gotta get hated
gotta get berated
it's the Mexican way of life
the park always brings out
the worse in Andres Sobaco

DOS AMIGOS

Sobaco's friend was fat and bald
and eyed girls with sad intent
he dreamed of being rich and skinny
Sobaco didn't bat an eye
life had passed them both by
but at least Sobaco knew it
his friend was lost and never found
nobody ever claimed you on the Westside
when the dust settled
it settled on dust
the silver-lining of clouds
was polished lead
when it rained it poured
but it was mostly mud
Sobaco's friend was fat and bald
and not even tall
Sobaco had seen it all
but that was not enough

HOMELESS

In another life Sobaco roams the city
homeless and held down
his shoes do not lack character
his walk is copyrighted
his smile lacks a smile
the skyline of San Antonio
could be on another planet
as far as Sobaco is concerned
the wind digs a hole
the sun rolls off his tongue
who are we kidding here
Sobaco picks up dust
from the sidewalk
examines it
puts it back
his grocery cart is a thing of art
Sobaco turns the corner hard
before he leaves the barrio
the monitor of his race

BABY SOBAQUITO

Sobaco's cloth diapers hanging on the clothesline
baby Sobaco crying for a breast to suck on
his mother washing the few dishes
the soapy water God had cast out of paradise
the forbidden fruit passed by like a train
the clickety-clack of fur
clouds knocking on the roof
which needed repairs
afterwards baby Sobaco
slept like a log
kicking his covers off
he dreamed he was delicious
in his old age Sobaco
did not remember being a baby
though he acted like one sometimes
we've come full circle
baby shit

FOR ALL THEY WERE WORTH

Andres Sobaco had man boobs
they jiggled when he walked
you could see them under his t-shirt
battling for all they were worth
the man had no shame
his cousins thought him crude
white people thought him rude
he was proud of them
like a well-endowed
middle school girl
his hairy nipples
were beginning to turn gray now
they sagged more and more
like his abuela's tits
Andres Sobaco had man boobs
they rubbed against the world
like a girl

ASLEEP INSIDE AN OLD GUITAR

Andres Sobaco el Numbnuts was too fat
to sleep inside an old guitar
even a grand piano would be a tight fit
the guitar crushed and splintered
the piano strings hit him
in his fat sweaty eyes
a cut above the left eye
a musical bruise on his belly
the keys that open nothing
in this black and white world
no room for the color brown
in the morning the piano
lies on the floor flat as paper
the only music is Sobaco's snoring
a Mozart fart Beethoven cloven
godforsaken music in arrears

TOTAL ECLIPSE OF THE SUN

The eclipse failed to cover up
Sobaco's big fat ass
he made fun
of the moon and sun
the total eclipse of his buns
had failed to materialize
maybe if Uranus
came between earth and sun
Sobaco laughed
and pulled up
his size 52 pants
the sunburn on his cheeks
lasted for weeks
photos of his partially eclipsed ass
showed up on Facebook
Google maps paused over the Westside
Sobaco flat on his belly
in his weed-infested backyard
could be clearly seen from space
his big naked ass
reflecting sunlight like glass

A MAN FOR ALL SEASONS

Andres "El Gordo" Sobaco
was a man for all seasons
you couldn't pin him down
you couldn't hold him up
all the king's horses
and all the king's forklifts
couldn't pry the seasons off of him
spring winter fall summer
his life was a bummer
but the Westside was nothing
without his fat ass
out and about
in his two-tone
bad to the bone Chevy
a car for all seasons
the radio blaring and sharing
indeed El Gordo panzon
was a man for all the wrong reasons

FIRE WITH FIRE

While most people fight fire with fire
Sobaco fought fire with wood
he fought floods by turning on the faucets
he fought off knife attacks
with his chubby chest
he fought off gun fights
by leading with his head
so as you can see
Sobaco is nobody's fool
his spur of the moment acts
are well-thought out
the neighbors shake their heads
strangers look at him
with confused looks
and walk away perplexed
under stress Sobaco's most relaxed

SIR MEX A LOT

Oh, my God Becky, look at his butt
it is so big, it looks
like a black girl's butt
I mean his butt is just so big
I can't believe it's so round and flabby
I mean it's gross
look he's just so goddamn brown
Sobaco never heard them talking
Sobaco just kept on walking
his buttcrack all sweaty
listening to Black Betty
going to the tienda
he was a big spenda
girl if you think his butt is big
you oughta see his belly
peanut butter and jelly
his underarms are smelly
Oh, my God Becky, look at his butt
it is so big, it looks
like a black girl's butt

THE HEAVY WEIGHT OF AMERICA

The heavy weight of America
surrounds the Westside
with its melted dream
dogs sniff at it and pass by
Sobaco kicks the dream aside
but it sticks to his shoe
what a sticky mess
this country has become
Sobaco just wipes it away
only the smell of shit remains
the smell of shit
that has become white man's America
Sobaco seems unconcerned
as he walks to the bus stop
on what used to be Martin Street
his belly undulating
like a wave out at sea
Sobaco making the bus lean
to one side as he boards it
Sobaco's ass takes up two seats

LAST MAN ON EARTH

If Andres Sobaco was the last man on earth
he would still live on the Westside
amid the decaying town
the Alamo sacred to no one
the San Antonio River
just a place to draw water from
and trek back to the Westside
the Tower swaying in the hot
empty winds which prevailed
the few birds which survived
refused to sing in their anger
stray dogs picked up stones
cats refused to bury their shit
a lion roamed the cliffs
by the crumbling Trinity University
Sobaco continued to sit
on his front porch
contemplating the few things left
to be contemplated
somebody had to do it
too bad it had to be him

THE WAKE

As he knelt and crossed himself
Sobaco was thinking
" There but for the grace of God go I."
and in the coffin
his dead friend's only thought was
" I'd rather be dead
than be Andres Sobaco."
So there you go, gente
life and death
can have a such a powerful effect on us
Sobaco offered his condolences to the widow
and to the widow's daughter
whose little black dress
exposed her thighs
which sent Sobaco reeling
and covering his head
in case God sent a lightning bolt his way
and didn't miss this time
like God had missed
so many times before
maybe God was just getting old

SEPTEMBER 11

Andres Sobaco was chillin
Andres Sobaco was willin
Andres Sobaco was reelin
the planes struck
the planes snuck
the towers shook
look look look
the towers burned and fell
the smoke and smell
America stood still
will it recover it will
will it ever be the same
only in name
Andres Sobaco went out on his porch
to see if Miss Liberty still held the torch
he couldn't see it from the Westside
where only the brave reside
Andres Sobaco was reelin

GOOD MORNING VIETNAM

Good Morning Vietnam shouted Robin Williams
and a part of Sobaco's past
rolled like a rock inside his head
too fat to join the Army
even if had wanted to
Sobaco spent the Vietnam War
proudly serving the Westside
eating and sleeping
and watching the news
which everyday announced
how many American soldiers
had needlessly died that day
Sobaco was patriotic to his Westside
Sobaco was no coward
and being Mexican proved it
Sobaco sat on his crumbling porch
drank his beer like poison
and soldiered on

CLEANING THE BEANS

Sobaco was cleaning the stones
out of the pinto beans
once he had neglected to clean them good
and he'd bit down
and broken one of the few teeth
he had left
life's a bitch and then you die
shouted Sobaco to no one in particular
in the sweltering kitchen
while outside the kitchen window
the sky was dark brown
the sun limped along
like Don Urias
picking up aluminum cans
Don Urias had a hot great-granddaughter
who often strutted by Sobaco's house
as if she owned the world and all the beans
Sobaco could eat and fart

WELCOME TO THE JUNGLE

3 am and Sobaco's crazy neighbor
screams like a banshee
no doubt swinging his arms like a beast
welcome to the jungle
junkyard for the race
which once built pyramids
and cut out hearts
nothing has really changed
Mexicans build everything
in this godforsaken beautiful town
and cut out each other's hearts
in the hot smoky cantinas
Sobaco lays back down
dreams of panocha
and other delicacies
growing wild on the Westside

BORRACHOS

All night long the borrachos drank
beer after beer cigarette after cigarette
conjunto music filled the air
like dark clouds
the sound carried up and down the street
wrinkled out ladies snored soundly
just a few blocks away
the neighborhood punks
bitched about the borrachos
the cops hung out ten blocks away
drinking black coffee and boredom
the prostitute had called it quits hours ago
slouching towards Bethlehem Street
Sobaco slept soundly too
dreams spilling out of his mouth
onto the yellow pillow case
as if they were in a hurry to get out

NIGHT OUT

Sobaco's friends were dark as night
tossed like a coin they were neither heads nor tails
at the Westside bars they were light bulbs
down at the river bars
they were like sand in an hourglass
Sobaco drank the foam
and left the beer stand
the pretty girls were all pretty
and beyond his grasp
his friends whistled like wolves
to no avail
hit the trail
said the girl's tails
the river rafts dragged bottom
the tourists didn't have a clue
the buildings rose like toes
on Gulliver's feet
Sobaco's friends looked like ants
Sobaco woke up on the floor
in t-shirt and pants

BARRIO BLUES

One morning Sobaco's balls sagged
like American democracy
the Bill of Rights stirred itself in semen
the Statue of Liberty
breathed a sigh of relief
before going back to sucking
on Sobaco's soul
you see America ain't that bad at all
there's still hope
inside those purple mountain majesties
well maybe not on the Westside
but elsewhere yes elsewhere
Sobaco wakes up from the American Dream
the barrio is so real it hurts
the barrio pokes a finger in Sobaco's face
the barrio spits on Sobaco
Sobaco smiles and cries
"Oh, my lovely barrio,
how can I live without you?"

GROCERO'S GROCERY STORE

Andres Sobaco's underarms repel
the ladies at Grocero's Grocery Store
deep in the barrio's ass
he's buying beer and beans
a sack of potatoes
and a cardboard can of oatmeal
he pays
and leaves his armpit calling card behind
he walks the seven blocks home
no use in wasting gas
anyway his car has been sputtering lately
its horses laying down caballos
he pops a beer can open
sits on his porch like a torch
doesn't stop until everything is scorched

SOBACO'S BARRIO

Sobaco's barrio is not a barrio anymore

the old ones have died

and the young ones have moved away

Resendez Grocery Store is no more no hope

Munche's Store sinks lower and lower

into the past

the swings at Blumberg Park

sit on the ground without chains

the new kids on the block

don't even have a cock

an ancient one or two

still refuse to die

but Sobaco's barrio

is not a barrio anymore

SOBACO'S ABUELO

Sobaco's abuelo was a keeper
worked hard drank hard
played hard died hard
Sobaco inherited none of that
his fat ass barely lifted a finger
to shoot the bird
but Sobaco had hidden charm
what that was nobody knows
he went through life
by going through life
Sobaco's abuelo fought hard
dove into life battled life
loved life chased life
through the running barrio
Sobaco would never be an abuelo
thank God y Dios tambien
y La Virgen de Guadalupe of course
can't forget her, can we, Carmen?

ESPEJO

Andres Sobaco was honey in a mirror

to the widow Lomas

a bystander would certainly utter

"How disgusting!"

the nosy vecinas

would be vituperative

children in dirty underwear

would not care

the widow Lomas

would pamper her loins afterwards

sometimes sex is all we have

the mirror will not come clean

let it stay sweet

no matter how much

it bothers us

THE ICEHOUSE DRIVE INN

The maricon who hung out
at the Icehouse Drive Inn in Bermuda shorts
whistled at a stray dog
which stood on the hot asphalt
asphalt so old it had become a fossil
Sobaco bought his beer
chips and cigarettes
it's better never to look back
or forward thought Sobaco
as his mind tumbled
in and out of traffic
a city bus the size
of a brontosaurus
blocked the intersection with its tail
Sobaco's belly sweated profusely
the sky fit like underwear
and the sun let out a squeak
as Sobaco walked into his house
it's just a mouse
life is a louse

STRANGERS IN THE NIGHT

Strangers in the night
hate at first sight
outside the Icehouse Drive Inn
two cabrones looking for a way out
pistols knives knuckles
define a pendejo in the barrio
one was buying bread
the other beer like Sobaco
Sobaco sat down on the picnic table
which had names and initials
carved all over it
he watched the two idiots
battle it out
one kicked while the other one swung
both left bloody and torn
slices of bread on the ground
beer cans on the cement
free for the taking
strangers in the night
not what Frank meant

TURN ON YOUR LOVE LIGHTS, WESTSIDE

When Andres Sobaco turns on his love light
the light bulbs blow up with a pop
and the shattered glass lands on his head
forget about it
no train entering a tunnel
on the dusty Westside
no vieja tonight
the moonlight wasted
the stars' useless pricks of light
the planets circle their wagons
and Andres Sobaco is demoted like Pluto
poor lonely puto

THE FALLACY OF DAIQUIRIS

Sobaco's mind was clear as a bell
well maybe it had a crack in it
like the Liberty Bell
maybe it had a crack in it
like the whole damn country
but from the Westside
he couldn't see it
everything seemed perfect to him
the Mexican Dream
had replaced the American Dream
and Sobaco's fat ass
bounces through the barrio
convinced the Westside is paradise
and only if he keeps his eyes
closed long enough
will one tequila tell the other the truth

INTO THE SUNSET

When Sobaco walks into the sunset
his rounded shadow
stretches back into the Westside
the barrio darkens and flickers
before it goes dark for the night
Sobaco's heavy breathing echoes
in the alleys and the trash can lids
ring like cymbals
dogs sniff right and left
cats blacken against the night
Sobaco is only a memory now
a man with no particular gift
a man devoid of talent
the sunset pays him no mind
all we see is Sobaco's fat behind
life is more than you can ask for

BOOK TWO

EL OCHO PATAS

Arturo Sandoval was born with eight feet. The doctors wanted to do corrective surgery but his mother refused, saying that it was God's will. In school the Mexican kids called him El Ocho Patas. Eight Feet. White kids called him Spider. But to us, he will always be known as El Ocho Patas.

EL OCHO PATAS

If you must know
my mother was a spider
(joking of course)

she dug up
tortillas in the backyard

my barrio was stolen
by a girl in trenzas

my cousin
took all the trees

the police arrested
the color brown

my mother
spun her web

caught
her sons

the wind
would bring its knife to shake us blue

the barrio got by
with what gente it could

and if you must know
I spit like a spider too

UN TRIP TO THE OUTLET MALL

El ocho patas
went to the outlet mall

looking
for chavas

the young girls in shorts
always in demand

and there were
too many sunglasses for sale

the food court
didn't sell real tacos

and the Indian fellow
was yellow

the custodian
was Cambodian

el ocho patas
scattered everywhere

ANDABA A GATAS

El ocho patas
andaba a gatas

crawled
like a baby

his generation
was ashamed of him

never tied his ocho zapatos
he pawed his sentences

might lose
a pata or two

he might not
jump as high

but you can see it
in his eyes

he might as well have
ocho ojos

to see
pendejos

CASA DEL OCHO PATAS

Walls, floors,
lamps, bricks, dirt

buses, skyscrapers
el ocho patas could live anywhere

hasta en la cabeza
de un dinosaur

hiding in broom closets
to scare muchachas

or the mujeringos
a chingos

hasta en las casas de superheroes
el ocho vivia

era muy resourceful
como era mejicano

era un mejicano malo
y bueno what's the difference

el ocho patas
puede vivir en tu mente gente

EL GARRAPATAS

Like a garrapata
he clung to her

thinking that love
was a real thing

como una cola
the buey

believed in the American way
and the American way

no lo queria
so when el ocho patas

kicked your ass
you knew it

his ocho corazones
broken by a girl

he cried spider tears
in a dark closet

el mero mero
brown recluse

MOON WALKING PATAS

El ocho patas
was one hell of a dancer

moon walking
on all the moons of Mars at once

una corbata
de lata

mistaking pearls
for girls

he danced up a storm
danced hip hop to polka

his camaradas
put a cape over his shoulders

como si fuera
James Brown

a rodillas
a rodillas

the applause was deafening
to his ocho orejas

THE YOUNG OCHO

She lived on the
ocho calles of Seguin

the lawless town
which floated above it

singing its pan de dulce
above her house

her skinny legs
filled with desire

the police car
wore a carnation

ocho
was popping fireworks in his youth

against the ancient sea
which still made noise

along College Street
and flooded the library

where el ocho patas
had once had two fake feet

OCHO BUSTED HIS HEAD AGAINST HIS OWN HEAD

Ocho always saw the truth
but the truth rarely saw him

and so they butted heads
each in their own minds

assumed the win
como piedra contra piedra

ravaging river
against river bank

tall building
against tall building

and Ocho walked
between fire and ice

while the barrio children
fought lice

and white people
fought brown children

Ocho spoke the truth
but the world would only accept lies

and who's to say
the world was wrong

HIJO SOBREVIVIENTE DE LA LLORONA

El ocho patas
lived in the past

and he lived
in the future

the present
was only temporary

dia y noche
eran coche

he would write
poesia

because he hated
poetry

he hated
palabras

which could only be handled
like a cup of muddy water

the present
was only to be tasted

allí

en el arroyo

SPIDER VATO

Ocho was born with
super weaknesses

which made him strong
un cabron muy fuerte

he had a heart
of fool's gold

able to leap tall buildings
inside an elevator

could spin his web
to catch the insects of man

and the moths
of women

he traded in
his red white and blue

for ocho
calcetines rotos

ABUELA DE OCHO

El ocho ate his beans
tall tortillas at the ready

he remembered his abuela
always telling him

never fight
harder than you have to

there's a limit
to what effort

there are roads
you do not need

bridges built
for no rhyme or reason

birds that
do not need to fly

but el ocho patas
spun his wheels

thinking that abuela
would not approve

SCARECROW

El ocho's alter ego
was made of trigo

back in the day
when el ceso

was not considered
progreso

and el ocho's heart
was just the start

does it now surprise you
that el ocho loved a woman

in all the correct places
even in her faces

and he loved words
como si fueran palabras

the wind blowing inside a bell
el ocho has come a long way

blazing the trail
like tortoise and snail

with the wink of an eye

of course

THE ROOTS

El ocho patas crossed the border
before it became fashionable

before America became
so self-righteous

and self-centered
el ocho patas

made himself at home
grew roots

reached for the stars
and burned his hands

picked pecans
and cotton

before America
became rotten

el ocho patas
could be quite a handful

FLYING PATAS

El ocho patas volaba
the first of his kind

took to the sky
surprising la raza

from pachuco roots
or in cahoots

turbo-charged wings
over the barrio

lowriders
ain't got a chance

los deja
sin pants

and el otro patas
flew too close to the sun

and the sun
fell to the ground

PATA'S JOB

El ocho patas went about his job
eight patas at a time

some poems were rats
some were cats

pero si esperas un rato
the next line will not rhyme

el ocho was trigger happy
when it came to writing it down

the new lines
always at his toes

silence at the tip
of his tongue

his fingertips
waiting

el ocho patas was quite clever
the way he pulled the lever

EL CUATRO

A veces hacia tricks
he'd walk on four feet

of his left side
it made the girls giggle

the men just said
what a show off

but el ocho
or should we say el cuatro

had more tricks
up his pant legs

the cabron
could even walk on two feet

that being quite a feat
even for a man

THE MAGICIAN'S ASSISTANT

El ocho patas
cut the magician's pretty assistant in half

while the magician
jumped up and down

screaming profanities
and the audience went wild

thinking it was
part of the show

el ocho patas
had one regret

that the girl
had only two legs

but he had to make do
with what he had

after all
el ocho patas

was put on this earth
to work his magic

THE RAINS CAME

The rains came
el ocho patas swam

the thunder clapped
and so did el ocho

la Llorona was screaming
by the arroyo

the police charged her
with disorderly conduct

they did not see
her children bobbing up and down

the rains came
el ocho patas swam

this is not who I am
he kept saying

no one heard him
in the rain

La Llorona rotted
in an American jail

the rains came

el ocho patas swam

THE GREAT CREATOR

El ocho patas
often thinks that

the great creator
is a faker

much like himself
and you

yes you
right here

in front of me
says el ocho patas

he can see
right through you

because he can see
right through himself

you can't hide the truth
from the truth

you can't rely
on a lie

como si para siempre

fuera forever

OCHO IN LOVE

El ocho patas was in love
and his patas got in the way

long walks on the beach
turned into hurricanes

moonlit nights
turned into fights

his girl held his patas passionately
it must be love he thought

too many shoes to buy
left little money to buy her a ring

but somehow he bought her a wedding ring
and eight for him

eight children they would certainly have
oh what a tangled web we weave

PYRAMID OF THE PATAS

When el ocho patas
climbed the Pyramid of the Sun

he made it
look so easy

the tourists
stared in awe

the locals
tried to figure out

how to make money
from Ocho's talent

the stupid teenagers
were unimpressed

a mangy dog
tilted its head sideways

a crazy thought
jiggled in his canine mind

like a girl jogging topless
on a faraway beach

CUMBIA

La muchacha danced a polca
with her boca

to impress
al ocho patas

polca
que revolca

el ocho patas
takes off his zapatos

kisses the muchacha
aunque sea gabacha

el parche
plays the blues in a smoky cantina

it will be my ruina
he sings

la muchacha dances
for all her ass is worth

and el ocho patas cumbias
as if he has no patas

EL OCHO VACAS

El ocho patas
pretended to be a real poet

and the idiot public
believed him

hook line and sinker
pescados

and sure
el ocho patas

was indeed guilty
of pecados

so there must be
a little pleasure in evil he thought

as he went about his way
the bell around his neck

ringing in the meadow
where the wild flowers copulated

thorn against thorn
petal against petal

even if you're not a cow
you can still be a vaca

KNEW A GIRL

El ocho patas knew a girl
he wanted to know

in the biblical nonsense
it did not matter

if it was just a sin
he imagined

filling up her long legs
spinning a web

around her waist
wasting nothing

oh the baby spiders
they would produce

out of lust
because apparently

that's what God
had intended

and who the hell
was ocho patas

to tell God

he was wrong

EL OCHO AMORES

El ocho patas was very fond of what
lies above a woman's patas

the smile the hair
it isn't fair

the coy glance
of her hardware and software

ravine with
no bridge

the sweetness
of her sourness

his ocho patas gritan
the better to love her with

to hold her
against eight moonlit noches

over and under the eight
Aztec and Mayan suns

el ocho patas
was such a romantic

MAD LOVE

El ocho patas wanted to be
madly in love

you know
like in the old days

not the worn out
kind of love

of course
that was foolish of him

and being an old fool
only made it worse

his heart made of hay
was blown about by the wind

his heart made of flesh
still hungered for desire

his lion's mane
flickering

his sharp claws
dancing

el ocho patas
could feel the mad love

as he held her
against his own will

OCHO CLAVOS

El ocho patas
was hard as nails

you'd think
he was en la primavera

of his barrio life
cleansing las calles of muchachas

in the hot summer nights
the dust of the gravel streets

billowing into clouds
the moon rubbing its eyes

to see el ocho's shenanigans
a girl pulling up her past

like a 1951 Ford
pulling up to a stop sign

el ocho grinding gears
hard as nails

BOUNCING BENNY PATAS

El ocho patas
had taken liberties

with her luscious body
back in the day

when lust was still allowed
the cave

decorated with furs
stones hot from the fire

wild animals
peeked from behind bushes

scratched their scent
on boulders

her luscious body
didn't care about love

as el ocho patas
came from above

HIS PATA HAD BOTH SIDES

"Both of his sides are all the same
glows his grin with all but shame."
                      Berryman The Bridge Jumper

El ocho patas
struggled long and hard with his malady

his feet pushed away
and grasped towards

his contradiction in terms
was one and the same

the flies of God flew high
and they flew low

banging their heads
against angels

and dragging their feet
in the devil's poop

el ocho patas
fought long and hard

yet always succumbed
dumb

but look on the bright side he said

there's always the threat of sun

PATAS DE LA LLORONA

El ocho patas
was the arroyo

where La Llorona
drowned her children

mud rocks pebbles
weeds

all sorts of debris
made up el ocho patas

his eyes dodging
flotsam and jetsam

stormy rain
pounding his abdomen

el ocho patas
screamed at La Llorona

but himself the arroyo
was so loud

that nobody could hear anyone
just like you can't hear me now

DADDY LONG LEGS

for vangie vigil

El ocho patas
had once been a man

and even though
he was a spider now

he still thought
like a man

he chased
girl spiders

as if they were
going out of style

with a spring
to his eight feet

he stood
on a street corner

and admired
the passing beauties

his ocho patas

were not politically correct

and his mind

was always erect

LOOK MA NO HANDS

El ocho patas
ate with his feet

since he had
no hands

go ahead
laugh if you want

make fun
of him

his ocho patas
all muddied with food

refried beans
if you must know

you ask
why don't he eat flies

like a good
little spider

but el ocho patas
thinks he's a man

THE MUSICAL FRUIT

When el ocho patas
split the atom

the bean
came falling out

the caldo
was quite hot

there were
no silly

or strange quarks
like scientists

will lead you
to believe

only beans
make up the atom

let no one
tell you otherwise

THE RESCUE

El ocho patas
pulls La Llorona

from the San Antonio River
by her broken silver wings

her underwear
is muddy

her mouth
full of water

her hair
collects sticks and stones

tall buildings
leap into the sky

the Alamo
tells her its lies

el ocho patas
drags La Llorona

onto the banks
of the pointless

San Antonio River
and as she dries off

her breasts
harden on her chest

and she will not
thank him

LA MOSCA

El ocho patas
was eating a mosca

the juices
clung to his whiskers

he spit out
the convex eyes

el ocho patas
looked through the see-through wings

he let the mosca's feet
fall to the floor

the lady of the house
never had a clue

she vacuumed
them up

but her shaggy white carpet
only fooled Americans

CICADA GIRL

When el ocho patas
woke up

his ocho patas
remained asleep

deep in dream
or nightmare

the planet
shook like the sun

zebras
wasted water

a poetess
with thighs of whirlwind

dropped ocho's
beating heart

into a well
like a stone

when el ocho
finally woke up

there was enough of her

for everyone

EL MERO MERO MERO

To some
el ocho patas was a monster

to others
he was the apple of their eyes

his walk
was imitated by children

his eyes
terrified soccer mothers

some men admired
how he carried himself

lawmen cried
because their silly handcuffs

were useless
when it came to el ocho patas

el ocho
was oblivious to the commotion

long ago he'd accepted the fact
that he was a fact

BEAT POET

El ocho patas
beat a man to death with his poetry

and the audience
applauded

it even went so far
as to give him a standing ovation

it was really about time
poetry did something

to get itself
out of the hole

it had fallen into
through no fault of its own

but this killing
had worked wonders

and el ocho patas notes
that no one disagrees with him

THE SLAVE

El ocho patas
loved a slave

you know damn well
we still have them

in this free country
of ours

she was a woman
you would not suspect

of being
a slave

she was a girl
you would not think

was a slave
she was a girl child

you could not
fathom a slave

but yes
el ocho patas

loved such a slave

in your free country

HUEVOS RANCHEROS

El ocho patas
was bad to the bone

era muy
cabrón

only huevones
eat huevos rancheros

his ancestors
ate flies

huevos de mosca
to be more exact

let them cowpokes
choke on huevos rancheros

his ancestors
ate chapulines

huevos rancheros
ain't got nothing on them

have you ever seen them
jump off the plate

SELENA

And the three men
el ocho patas admired most

he, himself
and el mismo

caught the tren
for you know when

he met a girl
who would be killed

by a pinche vieja fea
but the girl's music would live on

even all the way
to el Japon

yet el ocho patas
thought only of himself

and those two other vatos
I already mentioned

so he went about his business
as if nothing had ever happened

porque his cosas

were muy sabrosas

QUETZALCOATL'S PATAS

El ocho patas
often thought of himself as Quetzalcoatl

he of the few feathers
but many huaraches

he tried to lead his raza
into the future

but they clung to the past
stuck in reverse

or what was worse
not moving at all

tiesos as if frozen
so el ocho patas

shook his head
and flew on ahead

his feathered feet
was all his raza ever saw of him

as they sank
and stank

with only themselves

to thank

HIS OBSESSION

(A perfume manufactured for
el ocho patas in the north of France)

His obsession
was half possession

he floated on the Aztec moon
just thinking of her

he razed the pyramids
in his mad desire

built yellow brick roads
leading to her house

el ocho patas
was dizzy for her

he longed
to have her body against his

her thighs
wrapped around his eight thighs

his sixteen shoe laces
in a knot on the floor

where her clothes had landed

in good taste

BROWN LIKE ME

Everybody was brown like me
but everybody avoided me

my barrio
didn't recognize me

I hurried nowhere
with my ocho patas

I bought tacos on Sunday
just like you

I went to the same
Westside bakery just like you

bought my conchas
and my empanadas just like you

but nobody accepted me
because of my eight feet

everybody was brown like me
but they couldn't be me

as I dragged my ocho patas to sleep
as I dragged my ocho patas to sleep

EL OCHO'S BIRTHDAY

El ocho patas
had a birthday

but nobody
bought him shoes

nobody bought
his books

nobody was
somebody

and yet
everybody was someone

except of course
for Juan

and Juana
and her sister Chana

who loved el ocho patas
once or twice

gave birth to a daughter
who cherished lice

nobody

can be more than somebody

you shouldn't handles

more than candles

BEATLE BOOTS

Back in the day
it was tough for his abuela

to buy eight Beatle boots
for the teenage ocho patas

since the pata family
was dirt poor

el ocho patas
had to brush his teeth

with rain water
and he had to swim miles to school

where he slept through classes
couldn't afford glasses

poverty had the whole familia
by its asses

but el ocho persevered
just as you feared

THE BEGINNING OF THE END

El ocho patas
and his dancing bear

planned to convert
the barrio into a circus

complete with
big tent

dirty circus hair
mistreated elephants

tigers sprayed with scalding water
psychotic chimps

and highwire girls
with voluptuous feet

but where to put
the Mexicans he wondered

where to put
the dusty streets

the greasy river
and then the bearded lady

made a suggestion
el ocho patas loved

and just like that
the barrio was no more

EL OCHO PATAS
PART TWO

LA MIGRA

El ocho patas
thought La Migra

was after him
but it turned out

to be las migas
you know

scrambled eggs
with sliced up

corn tortillas
diced onions

tomatoes
and cilantro

La Migra
don't come around

with any of that
so el ocho patas

breathed a sigh of relief
and ate his migas like a citizen

THE GOLDEN FLEAS

And so
el ocho patas

set off in search
of the golden fleas

battling a metal giant
along the way

high-pitched
screaming women

cyclops and lollipops
well maybe not lollipops

and when el ocho patas
and his patas did find

the golden fleas
well you know

the golden fleas bit the hell
out of ocho from head to argonuts

THE LYNCHING

They tried to lynch
al otro patas

on that old oak tree
by the square

in Seguin, Texas
just like

they had lynched
other Mexicans

they wanted to see
el ocho's ocho patas

swinging wildly
but instead

the rope snapped
and the always

faithful branch
splintered

and el ocho patas
dropped to the ground alive

and the sons of bitches
stood there motionless

and the oak tree shuddered
lost all its bark

and el ocho patas
lived on and on

SUPER OCHO

Abuela washed
el ocho's cape

somehow he got it
full of salsa

abuela washed
el ocho's calzoncillos

she washed
his super pantalones

she boiled
his frijolitos

hasta que el ocho
got panzon

and flew off
haphazardly

to date an unwed mother
I mean

to help the poor
aunque a huevo

EXTRA BOLA

So God
took one of el ocho's

three balls
and created woman

the psychological pain
it inflicted upon

Adan Ocho Patas
has haunted him

for a billion years
that's why

el ocho's brain
limps

and uses a cane
unable

to fulfill
his manly life---

God's not the
best creator

curses the mutilated

ocho macho

STAR TRACALADA

To think
that el ocho patas

had once believed
in revolution

and had grown
a mustache to prove it

and donned
a sombrero

wrote the
mandatory poems

about la raza
had praised

the barrio
re-invented abuelas

learned to speak
the Mexican lingo

but the revolution
did not materialize

the transporter malfunctioned

maybe Scotty was on the potty

DOOMSDAY

The doomsday asteroid
that hit

el ocho patas
on the head

and bounced off
into the Gulf of Mexico

had surprised NASA
el ocho had

a big welt on his head
for weeks afterwards

his memory
of the whole event

was fuzzy
to say the least

and the scarred earth
was no help

the asteroid
boiled under the sea

warm

as pee

but el ocho patas

recovered… see

TRASERO

The clouds question
ocho patas

high and mighty
they look down

upon his many feet
they guffaw and gossamer

across the sky
like crows

el ocho patas
does not care

even the sun
tries to ridicule him to no avail

the moon has
tried to blacken him to no avail

the stars have purposely
fallen upon him trying to harm him

but el ocho patas always turns
the other cheek the otra nalga

I SING THE BODY ELECTRIC

I sing the body electric
said el ocho patas

as he stuck his finger
into a light socket

you could see
his skeleton light up

and his hair
stood straight up

like wire
so he pulled his finger out

and then proceeded
to stick it back in

he sang the body electric
until the city

cut off his utilities
as is bound to happen

in a just
and free society

A MOTHER'S LOVE

El ocho's mother
made sure

that his ego
was made

solely from
his ombligo

there had to be
no doubt

that el ocho
would be

his own man
perhaps ignored

by most
but that

would give
him the strength

to create
his own weakness

SOL AZTECA

El ocho patas
took the Aztec sun

in one hand
and the ungrateful

ball of fire burned him
and this

after el ocho
and his people

had sacrificed
so much

for the
bright son of a bitch

how many
virgins had died

for it
how many hearts

had been
torn out in vain

el ocho grabbed the sun again
but this time with both hands

and crushed it
into charcoal

only then
was el ocho patas feliz

FRIDA HOLLOW

When el ocho patas
met Frida Hollow

he went inside
the echos were deafening

her walls
trembled like

Mexican earthquakes
her breasts

undulating
during the aftershocks

el ocho spewed
like El Popo

and the Aztecs
rose from the dead

wanting to build
more pyramids

el ocho
had to yell at them

no mas

no mas

but the echos

inside Frida

just confused

the hell out of everyone

and new useless

pyramids were built

in the shape

of Diego Rivera

I HEAR AMERICAN SINGING ITS CANCION

El ocho patas
heard America singing

while the carpenter's truck
was parked outside the beer joint

the mason was stealing bricks
from his bosses

the fisherman put holes
in a neighbor's boat

the shoemaker used cardboard
to mend high dollar shoes

the woodcutter chopped down
thousand-year-old trees

the young wife
cheated on her husband

el ocho patas
heard America singing

its two-faced song
all across the de-fruited plain

SUNGLASSES AT NIGHT

El ocho patas
wears his sunglasses at night

he can't see a damn thing
he can't see immigrants

he can't see poverty
he can't see the homeless

he can't see the rich
he can't see the devil

he can't see
La Virgen de Guadalupe

he can't see a damn thing
he's wearing his sunglasses at night

and it won't get any better
when daylight comes

THE HOUSE ON MANCO STREET

El ocho patas lived in the house
on Manco Street

it was full of sand
and cenizas

it was purple
en el distrito de los reyes

he lived there
with his eight feet

half of them
dipped into the dirty

San Antonio River
his eight socks

colored the river brown
eventually he left town

and Manco Street
limped into history

AMANDA

El ocho patas
loved a girl named Amanda

who lived
on this side of the moon

and Amanda's thighs
were troublesome

and her breasts
were tightly wound

her eyes were made
of stars

brighter than the headlights
of cars

el ocho patas loved
her madly

and he loved
her sadly

and the love they shared
was scared

they loved each other

like hate

THE BIG TIME

El ocho patas
finally made the big time

in a small way
of course

her wore the same
dull shirts

the same cheap
Rustler jeans

but in a big way
and at least

two new people
knew his famous name

but no one
came to his readings

his eight webbed feet
walked on water

but he was
just an otter

CHICANO CRASH TEST DUMMY

El ocho patas
was no dummy

in the true sense
of the word

and if he was
it was purely by accident

with his never give up
attitude

and his
savoir faire

his clairvoyance
and his voyclairance

the cabron
was no pendejo

in the true sense
of the word

and if he was
it was purely by pendejada

FEET FETISH

El ocho patas
was the sum of all men

same strengths
and weaknesses

same super powers
same faults

he dragged his eight feet
through mud

he poured the sand
out of his eight sneakers

he sought the same women
all men sought

he was capable of love
he was capable of hate

but he was
the only man

who could truly be
el ocho patas

hero an almighty
to his feet

LOVER'S KISS

He took her tongue
in his mouth

the look of her eyes
tightening in her thighs

fingers which sought
her soul

like a ship
in the night

finding treasure
so dangerous

in this life
and times

the kind of love
which surfaces

and floats at sea
like her knees

God so cunning and clever
in what he gave to flesh

ON THE COVER OF THE ROLLING STONE

El ocho patas
wrote about beauty

about truth
about justice

about impossible
Mexican girls

but he could never
get on the cover

of the Rolling Stone
el ocho patas

had his own
curandera

he had his own
chupacabra

his own damned raza
but he could never

get on the cover
of the Rolling Stone

CUATES

Once upon a time
the Lord Jesus

and el ocho patas
were one and the same

they preached love
and peace

but only hate
and violence

fell upon their heads
so el ocho patas

made a run for it
hightailed it

out of there
went his own way

two roads diverged
in a yellow wood

and el ocho
turned yellow

BICICLETA

El ocho patas
got on his anti-bicicleta

and went
anti-everywhere

nothing was there
and nobody cared

just the opposite
of what we couldn't think

our anti-shouting
was silencing

what we had not learned
we forgot

the anti-bicicleta
parked outside Carmen's house

waiting for her
not to come out

waiting not to give her a ride
on the anti-handlebars

CAPE CANAVERAL

El ocho patas
blasted off from Cape Canaveral

his ass shooting
flames and smoke

his mind
headed to the stars

his big ears flapping
in the wind

his eight feet
swinging wildly

in eight directions
ready to spread

his wings on the moon
claim the land

for those of his kind
so long planeta

come visit me soon
he shouts from the moon

burnt out rocket
still in his pocket

AQUARENA SPRINGS

In another life
el ocho patas

was Ralph
the Swimming Pig

of Aquarena Springs
he entertained

the children
and the adults

who never grew up
and embarrassed

the boy pigs
and the girl pigs

swooned and
day dreamed

but alas one day
they closed Aquarena Springs

and Ralph drowned his sorrows
in the mud that was left

and which became

San Marcos, Texas

OTRA VEZ

El ocho
didn't believe in reincarnation

but the higher ups
or the lower downs

whichever
you prefer

preferred that el ocho patas
be brought back

in the form
of a millipede this time

in a previous life
el ocho had been a centipede

but of course he was unaware of that
though he had always favored

more than
two boring feet

FIGURE EIGHT

El ocho patas
the man

the myth
the legend

the hero
the anti-hero

the length
the width

the high
the low

shallow
and deep

socks
and calcetines

the eight shoes
that make you angry

that you love
more than the guy above

CHALECO

The naked girl
who lived inside the sun

was el ocho's
small-breasted girl

the pen knife
jumped up like a fish

a towel ganged up
in a dark barrio

el ocho's plump family
wore sunglasses

gold bubbled up
from his sister

el ocho had his life
squeezed into a mosquito

proud of burros
and polished sex

he kept his best
close to his chest

PATAMERICA

El ocho patas
being a real country

had states
and non-states

rivers and deserts
clowns carnivals

sandwiches
shoe stores

turtles in shells
and turtles without

coathangers
nickles

pennies from heaven
and hell

angels with tiny breasts
machos with male problems

in other words
el ocho patas

was a real country
with a real name

not at all
like this one

WHOSE WOOD WAS HARD

His girl was
lovely, dark and deep

the little caballito
must have thought him queer

with eight feet
and way too many toes

but she loved him
way too mucho mas

the woods they
trespassed in

were full of snow
and trees

his girl
was lovely, dark and deep

sometimes love is more
than knee-deep

SWEET AS A MEXICAN BAKERY

She was as sweet
as a Mexican bakery

her conchas
sugary and soft

her empanadas
lemony tasting

her tres leches
gave him a milk mustache

all the other sweets that
dwelled in her he devoured

he was a glutton for her love
he didn't need real food

she was open at all hours
of the day and night

the girl behind the counter
rang up his weaknesses

the weaknesses
of men and marranitos

she was as sweet
as a Mexican bakery

SONGBIRDS

El ocho patas
rounded up all the birds

and got them
to sing a song for his beloved

they obliged
promised to leave their fleas behind

they sang the songs
their ancestors sang

before so many trees
were cut down

and replaced
with telephone wires

she cherished the songs
and made love

to el ocho patas
her underpants hummed on the floor

HOLLYWOOD SIGN

El ocho patas
wanted to be

a famous movie star
like Peckory Greg

but his dyslexia
held him back

nonetheless his career
never got down from the sky

as he lumbered
thru Hollywood

not even getting a commercial
for Preparation Hispanic

LA MERA MERA

El ocho patas
loved a woman who had guts

he loved her brown
lightning hair

her eyes
which flung fireballs

her hips
which exhausted his hands

her lips
which sang in his head like cactus

if she played with blood
that was fine

if she broke church bells open
so be it

if she ripped in love
well that was guts and glory

YOUNG LOVE

She claimed she was too young
to make love

rat that he was
he strutted his tail

his whiskers were wonderful
nonetheless

and she hugged him
like sticks on fire

she took off her bra
and flushed it down the toilet

she wrapped her panties
in aluminum foil

rat that he was
he gnawed at her sweet little throat

while the planet
slipped from its bedrock

and its gears
were laid bare

LA MADRE

When el ocho cried for his mother
she broke if she spoke

his shiny head
went on ahead

his heart was a tin can
he got old like air

when the arroyo
played with pebbles as stones

when the sun
skipped a day it was good

from the portholes
el ocho spilled the sea

creation had no heart
he thought

with his head in his hands
he cried for his mother's breasts

that they be saved
like the rest of us

SON OF GOD

El ocho patas
was God's son

he screwed
men women and children

he ate babies
and beauties alike

he didn't
pull any punches

he cheated
and lied

he was a coward
and a thief

not every son of God
has been as well shod

ARROYO

El ocho patas
was sure he could fix the arroyo

with pliers
and wrenches

or a martillazos
if need be

fix the damn thing
so no children could be thrown into it

by some despondent
Aztec princess

or some drug-crazed
Westside unwed mother

or some tattooed teenage father
bent on revenge

el ocho worked day and night
to repair the arroyo

but in the end
it was no longer an arroyo

and it reared up
on its hind legs

THIS IS YOUR CAPTAIN SPEAKING

This is your Captain speaking
said el ocho patas

though of course
he really wasn't

as the plane lifted
from Papalote

full of helote
into the crispy sky

of the two-timing Texas
and el ocho

kept pretending
to be the Captain

Ladies and Gentlemen
if you look out

the right side
of the plane

those hills there
that's where

in just about a minute

we will crash

BEAUTY AND THE BEAST

El ocho patas
loved a girl

and she
loved him

he was a beast
and she was beautiful

the ingrown toenails
of his patitas

did not compare
to her tetitas

love is blind
they say

and cannot smell
so well

when ocho bought shoes
she held his hand

as the crowd gathered
like sand

WHY BROWN BOYS DIE

El ocho patas
knows why brown boys die

shot while they walk
in the hood

while they ride in cars
down the street

while they buy cigarettes
at Family Mart

while they talk
to brown girls

while the sun
beats down on them

while the rains
soak their bandanas

while they proclaim
their macho ways

while they run
and jump over fences at night

when they trespass
on apartment complexes not their own

when they breathe
somebody else's gang-related air

while they stand on the corner
to cross the street into the beyond

el ocho patas
knows why brown boys die

SOME MEN

Some men aspire to greatness
el ocho just aspired

some men make dreams come true
el ocho doesn't dream

some men can always be trusted
el ocho only so far

some men are gentlemen
el ocho's just a man

some men are good with children
el ocho's just a child

some men respect all women
el ocho draws the line

some men rise to the occasion
el ocho goes on vacation

some men can see the future
el ocho sees the past

IN HIS OLD AGE

In his old age
el ocho patas became allergic

to beans
he became allergic

to corn and flour tortillas
he broke out in hives

if he ate conchas
or any kind of panochitas

or whatever it is
you call that sweet stuff

peddled by Mexican bakeries
so in his old age

after his vieja left him
he was left with no alternative

but to eat gringo food
you know sandwiches

yes old age
made him allergic to being Mexican

EL SANTO CANTO

El ocho patas was no saint
you could paint

he had a moat
around his throat

his angel wings
were just things

his kingdom by the sea
was full of pee

his queen
was not clean

still el ocho was a savior
a godly slayer

his eyes were dark
like a spark

he lived in a part of town
you could drown

he flew with birds
dropped turds

he was the patron saint
of ain't

ASH WEDNESDAY

At the end of a spear
el ocho patas squirms

just as you would
a bonfire with his name on it

a steady wind
blowing out of the south pole

a vicious girl scout troop
chanting his name

ocho ocho ocho ocho
until even the troop leader

throws up
at el ocho's eighty feet

el ocho burns well
his skin shriveling up

the smell of his burnt hair
pleasing all who have come to see him

light up their boring lives
the spearhead hangs in the air

for a moment

before it falls into the ashes

LOW DOWN

El ocho patas was
a low down dirty dog

his tail wagged him
his tail was his head

his head was
low down and dirty

he chased cats
eight invisible feet

he threw them off the bridge
with Bobbie Magee

he was a low-down dirty dog
all the girls wanted him

until they became women
and wanted a mind of their own

el ocho disowned them
his bite was worse than man

INAPPROPRIATE TOUCHING

El ocho patas was accused
of inappropriately touching the earth

the cops were notified
the Department of Earthly Welfare

was up in arms
el ocho was accused

of raping the earth's oceans
of fondling the earth's forests

of ejaculating on the earth's rivers
he was accused of having

sexual relations with an
underaged earth

the earth was after all
too damn young

only eight thousand years old
el ocho patas got life

ESTADOS UNIDOS DE VAQUEROS

El ocho lived in a funny country
it wanted everything done onto others

but not unto itself
so el ocho patas laughed

and poked fun
at his silly country

he ran circles around
his country's confused logic

those who ruled the airwaves
hated el ocho patas

and ridiculed his eight feet
but el ocho

made a running joke
out of his country

its big patriotic clown shoes
its big red rubber nose

HE CARRIED HER FEET IN HIS FEET

El ocho patas
carried her feet in his feet

his feet smelled
and hers were sweet

it was love
at first meet

they were love birds
tweet tweet

and everywhere
el ocho patas walked

her two little feet
copied the feat

and if el ocho fell
well hell

she fell too
black and blue they got up two

when they had made
enough of love

he carried her feet

in his feet

CANCIONES
DESGRACIADAS

"Pa todas las viejas que no me dieron su culo!" Toast overheard at a cantina frequented by my abuelo.

HUEVOS

I teach her how to play with my huevos
I tell her to scramble them
I suck her tongue out of her mouth
the game of love and desayuno

the ins and outs of the night
I squeeze her nalgas
I kiss her corazones
maybe I'm still a baby
maybe I still soil my diapers
after all I am only a man
I teach her how to play with my huevos

PERRO

She tells me I'm as hot
as a jalapeño
outside the Mexican restaurant
where a dog begs for scraps
and is disgusted
by my beer belly

perks up his ears
as he looks at my new girlfriend
who's a little gordita
and wonders why his own ribs
so visible to the world
elicit no goddamn pity whatsoever
and I think to myself
what gives this mangy dog
the right to judge a man

RANCHERA

I was eating my ranchera
who happened to be a güera
the Mexican restaurant had a patio
outside and afuera

I was eating my güerita
she said mañana I said horita
the restaurant Mariachis played a song
while I tugged on her thong

I was eating my gringuita
when she demanded all my salsa
she begged for the whole enchilada
so I gave her a nalgada

I was eating my ranchera
who happened to be a güera
she was paying for her ancestor's crimes
with her beautiful behind

RED WHEELBARROW

I stole that red wheelbarrow

glazed with rain

beside the white chickens

and I stole the chickens too

had my abuela cook them up

sold the wheelbarrow at the pulga

who says crime don't pay

HOWL

The small coins of her blue eyes
at the barbecue or at the rodeo
spin to a stop on the bed
when we get home
I am the wolf in sheep's clothing
my fur brown around the butt
what do you expect
I am a wild animal
and my instincts suck
I make love to her and howl
I am the best mind of my generation

COLON

Christopher dressed in a
white t-shirt and jeans was reciting
her poetry in the environs of the big city
to other big city cats who meowed
with the best and the worst as is always
the case when you think you're a poet
among poets but only poetry decides who's
for real and who's not for real
it's a cruel business which sucks
the life out of your heart and ass

AZTEC LOVER

She was my Aztec lover
she pulled my heart from my chest
she held my still-beating heart in her hand
her hand dripping with my hot blood

for a few moments I could feel
my hollow chest
the emptiness hurt
she looked at me
and with tears in her eyes she said
I love you too much and I am making sure
you never love anyone else
and suddenly I could feel my heart again
beating in her beautiful brown hands

TAMALES

Love is not all about the tamales she said
as she tore open my shirt
the buttons falling on the floor
making button noises
her fingernails raking my chest
as if she was raking leaves
and we don't even have a tree
in the whole damn barrio
where at night bullets fly like birds
where when the neighbor beats his wife
it sounds like a woodpecker
pecking away at a telephone pole

after our lovemaking has exhausted itself
the corn leaves lie on the floor
next to her panties

AUTHENTIC MEXICAN FOOD

My girlfriend offered me arroz con pollo

I told her I preferred her pozo de ole

she smiled and said

you can have that tonight

and I said what about dessert

she smiled and said

you can have some of my concha

and eat it too

YOU WANNA HEAR ABOUT LUPITO

Lupito got twenty years
for robbing the bakery on Martin Street
and for hitting the viejita
across the face
with the back of his tattooed hand
the one his Uncle Pancho
held him down by
while he performed
those vile acts on ten year old Lupito
those acts which rule
Lupito's life to this very day
not that that's an excuse
for what he did of course
his abuela called him
a sweet boy
and there you have it
Lupito's bitter life

JOSIE

Josie went to the dance Friday night

only her abuela called her Josefina

or sometimes Finita

aren't you going to eat something

before you go said her grandma

who always had warm tortillas

and beans or potatoes at the ready

as if she expected the apocalypse

Josie said no grandma

I'll get something to eat after the dance

Sunday they found Josie's body

in the San Antonio River

by one of the Spanish missions

besides the cause of death

which was blunt force trauma to the head

the medical examiner listed the contents

of her stomach

a partially digested burger

the gold cross she always wore

stuffed in her vagina

one of her thumbs missing

and yet even at the morgue

her soul still stood quietly next to her body

TERESITA

Teresita was nine years old
when a family friend raped her
her little brown eyes
were always the first thing
strangers would point out
as if they were pointing
to a shooting star
and just as quick
Teresita's innocence was taken
and though the rapist
got life in prison
Teresita got more than life

PEDRO LEOS

Killed by a drunk driver on Kingsbury Street
Pedro Leos still frequents those same bars
walking home drunk
swinging those arms which were part
of his personality and heart
his wife waiting at home
hoping he wouldn't spend
all his paycheck before he got home
she was dead too by now
and had no bills to pay
but the dead still have their worries

THE GREASY SPOON

Back in the Fifties
a greasy hamburger joint
posted a sign saying
Mexicans served around the back
niggers go down the road
to Emma's Place
but at least they had the courtesy
to tell you where to go
and abuelo pulled the perro
out of the stationwagon
and let him do his business
right at the front door
to greet the gringo customers
my abuelo was such
a forgiving man

ABUELO

Abuelo had his dark flaws
no he couldn't caw
he drank too much
and chased the ladies
las cantineras all dolled up
and ready to take his quarters
though abuelo was a hard worker
he was a tarnished penny
sometimes his life
wasn't worth a centavo
and he would always say al cabo
and you know what
his philosophy has stood the test of time

DESERT COWBOY

My father lived in the desert
like a Mexican gila monster
he took the sun in his mouth
and spit it out with the tobacco
he irrigated that damned desert
and its grapes of wrath
my father lost his wife and son
to that unforgiving hell
but he paid it back two-fold
from desert floor to mountain top
my father ruled with an iron hand
and now he's a handful of sand

SALTON SEA

After my mother died

my father took up with jealous women

they hated his kids and not one of them

was worth their weight in salt

not in the eyes of his grown kids

who swam the Salton Sea

from one side to the other

dodging Navy bombs

and saltwater sharks

they survived and forgave their father

for the sake of their mother

sometimes not everything is meant to be

DEEP IN THE BARRIO

Buried deep in the barrio
I dug myself out
my bruised hands
couldn't hold a tortilla
my mouth was full
of mother earth
the sun blinded my eyes
I squinted
trying to recognize my neighbors
their dirty faces
gave me hope
buried deep in the barrio
is not such a bad thing
it makes you sing

I REMEMBER ABUELO

I remember abuelo in a green and white
striped short-sleeve shirt
smoking a cigarette
as if it was yesterday
I remember abuelo holding a beer
the moisture on the bottle
the sun reflecting off of it
as he took a drink
I remember abuelo's thinning hair
as he brushed his hand over it
when he told a story or a joke
oh so long ago
like if it was yesterday
like if it was just yesterday

MACIAS BAKERY

My brothers were at Macias Bakery

when Macias came out to the front

my brothers asked him

how do you make such good pan dulce

and Macias blurted out

"pura manteca!"

a split second later

my brothers could see

his dark brown face turning red

after giving away trade secrets

and everytime we get together

we laugh our asses off

thinking Macias happy as hell

making cuernitos for the devil

THE MEXICAN BOY

When a boy loses his mother
it's devastating
but when a Mexican boy loses his mother
it's the end of the world
bundle up the trees and burn them
bottle up the rivers and bury them
tie up the clouds and box them up
bring down the sun and cover it with dirt
let the moon spin out of control
and bounce off the pain
that this Mexican boy
can never get rid of
even when he is dead
the pain is still there

PUMPKIN EMPANADAS

So I'm at the Mexican bakery and I tell the beautiful girl behind the counter that I want six pumpkin empanadas, two cuernitos four chocolate conchas, four cinnamon cookies, and two marranitos. As she's putting the empanadas in the box I tell her those don't look like pumpkin because the outside is glazed I tell her and your pumpkin empanadas aren't but she insists that they are indeed pumpkin so I pay and walk outside to my truck, open the box, crack open an empanada and sure enough they are pineapple empanadas, the most hated of all empanadas so I march back in and stand at the counter and unfortunately the same young Mexican girl walks up to me and I tell her, they are not pumpkin. She looks at the cracked empanada and still insists that they are pumpkin. Then another beautiful woman behind the counter hears our argument, she's in her thirties, fantastic smile and I wonder what she would be like in bed. Anyway she looks at the cracked open empanada and turns to the girl and says those are not pumpkin empanadas, they're pineapple, so she replaces my empanadas with pumpkin ones and I am the happiest Mexican in the whole wicked world.

NEW BARRIO BREASTS

Her new breasts barely the size
of a couple of cherry tomatoes
he sucked on and after he walked her home
he hoped he hadn't bruised them
or if he had he hoped her mother
did not see her without her t-shirt
the girl was eleven
she didn't understand her feelings yet
but she thought they were good
she relished them in secret
and told her fifteen year old boyfriend
she didn't feel a thing
she told him it was water
when it was really fire
and when she grew up
she wondered what's wrong with me
but it was too late
when it's been pounded in your head
at such a young age

FENCES

Back in the late 50's and early 60's
abuelo built barbed wire fences
that still stand today
strong as ever keeping back and out
whatever was meant to be
kept in check on Capote Road
there where the Guadalupe River
winds like a crooked snake
where we used to pick pecans as kids
fish along the gravel banks
swim to the tiny islands
the Guadalupe offered up as sand
as a treat to the young and old
the damn fences have outlived abuelo
and our childhoods as well

DEMONS

Abuelo fought demons all his life
he was not what he wanted to be
as a young man as a young buck
ready to shape the world
in his own Mexican image
spilling sons and daughters
out of his applauding groin
but soon the fire of ambition
turned to cold ashes
the aftermath of a black night
not one ember to poke at
only the reality that every Mexican
has to face sooner or later

THE HOUNDS OF HEAVEN

The hounds of heaven turned out

to be just chupacabras

who sniffed me circled me

and then disappeared into the darkness

that in a word is what is wrong

with us Mexicans

even the shit we make up

wants nothing to do with us

INSIDE A MEXICAN GIRL

These are the things I find
inside a modern Mexican girl
no more tortillas
no more tias
no more definitive abuelas
no more trips
to the tiendita
if she talks about the past
she means yesterday
she doesn't mean mañana
these are the things I find
inside a modern Mexican girl
too much barbecue
not enough barbacoa
too much mall
not enough pulga
too much later
not enough now
these are the things I find
inside a modern Mexican girl
the same damn Mexican girl
who always kicks my ass

HORMIGUERO

I'm done combing the Westside for ants
the dilapidated barrio houses
no longer suffer
old man Centeno's soul

cast aside like used gum
that won't stick to shoes
not even the ghost of ant mounds
spiral against dogs
who should know better

I'm done combing the Westside
for the sigh of ants
their little brown shoulders
I used to lean on

MARTIN STREET

Stray dog on Martin Street
eyes like a lost lover
the freeway humming like a bee
a cop strangles tacos

in days gone by
I ran up this Street
my long hair stretching
from Robert B. Green
the moon all sweaty in my hands
until I got to Cecilio's house
the San Antonio River
lies crumpled like newspaper
against a broken ancient curb
my tongue long as a sword

HEAD DOWN

Head down like a snake
I cross the Street
where I was raised
fruit which never ripens
calling itself a tree
the clouds stick to my pants
the wind round as a button
if I shed my skin upon your breasts
if my hair is the only thing
that holds up River Street
if I call your sweet name
with my rocks

THE SECRET OF LOVE

Your voice shakes like puppy legs
you clutch a pillow
to your goose-pimpled thighs
your heart is beating way too fast
outrunning light

that time you made a basket
playing in the winter league
at the rec center
your smile upon the shiny wooden floor
the janitor would not go near
love was not our menace then

MY CHIMP

My chimp is smoking up a storm

in the backyard to which

my girlfriend objects

as if I left the toilet seat up

or killed the ruffian

who mows our lawn

or the plumber whose ass hangs out

and works for himself

San Antonio ain't all

it's cracked up to be

MY SEGUIN

Remember when Guadalupe Street
ended just below Joe F. Saegert School
the drain pipe oozing into Walnut Creek
of course you don't
you weren't born yesterday
I was and I've dragged all those
memories around with me
until the day I die
and then my Seguin
the one that fills my head
will rise up into the sky
and fall back down with a crash
that everyone will hear
and then it will be your Seguin
to do with what you will

GALLO

When you hear a rooster
on the Westside being macho
and a punk in a bandana stands nowhere
when downtown the Tower
sways gently in the wind
and the river gathers its shallow depths
the cantinas open to let out the borrachos
I scurry like an ant on a leaf
trying to get back home
the rooster flaps its wings
amigo, we can soar but we can't fly

DANTE

I've been to hell

it's no better than heaven

the shit they feed you

the clothes you have to wear

speeches that praise

and berate

dust that comes

from who knows where

the servants suck

God's son can't fuck

I've been to hell

we're all out of luck

TONI

The giant ants have drifted
into town like a blue norther
and I remember sliding my finger
in Toni's panties
what was she maybe sixteen
maybe in between
I was lean
and what of these giant ants
which are looking for some sugar
like I was so long ago
they dig up Juan Seguin's grave
call him babe
make him a slave
I gotta cave
oh Toni

DUMP TRUCK

Mad at your house
there on Hidalgo Street
but we were just a ball of fire
in your mother's geraniums

making love in the arroyo
did not satisfy our thirst
the cops were looking
in the wrong place
we could hear them

my penis was a dump truck
oh to be a teenager again

SECOND GRADE

Ignacio back in second grade

life of the party

got all the Valentines

me the ugly duckling

dirty farm kid

poor as hell

didn't know how to spell

probably smelled

no running water at home

just the well

my family used to being poor

my father the sharecropper

my mother working in the fields

Ignacio back in second grade

me the ugly farm kid

never farmed a lick

waiting for the third grade

third degree

with bespectacled chubby Mr. Blumberg

STORM CLOUDS GATHER

Abuelo comes home drunk
and fucks abuela
for God's sake
I'm in the same damn room abuelo
my sister asleep

los vecinos
sending their son to Vietnam
so he can get killed

I'm holed up here
squeezing the rain
into my fist
I hear thunder in my knuckles
and the lightning
has no way to get out
I could do better

AUTHOR BIO

Reyes Cardenas was born and raised in Seguin, Texas. His books of poetry include, Survivors of the Chicano Titanic, I Was Never A Militant Chicano, and Chicano Poet-Poems 1970-2010.

www.ingramcontent.com/pod-product-compliance
Lightning Source LLC
Chambersburg PA
CBHW032125160426
43197CB00008B/513